Nazi Ideology

C. M. Vasey

Hamilton Books
A member of
The Rowman & Littlefield Publishing Group
Lanham • Boulder • New York • Toronto • Oxford

Copyright © 2006 by
Hamilton Books
4501 Forbes Boulevard
Suite 200
Lanham, Maryland 20706
Hamilton Books Acquisitions Department (301) 459-3366

PO Box 317
Oxford
OX2 9RU, UK

Library of Congress Control Number: 2005935200
ISBN-13: 978-0-7618-3343-7 (paperback : alk. paper)
ISBN-10: 0-7618-3343-9 (paperback : alk. paper)

Contents

Chapter One

Introduction

An ideology (Weltanschauung) can best be understood as a composite set of ideas, self-contained and self-reinforcing, which provide a distinctive outlook on the world. The most obvious political ideology is that of Marxism which, though there are many variants, is based upon an intellectual analysis of the nature of human development, drawing conclusions for the future structure of a desirable society from that analysis. But the rigorous intellectual analysis underpinning Marxism is totally lacking in the ideas that made up National Socialism. Nazism" or "National Socialism" (Nationalsozialismus) refers to the politics of the dictatorship which ruled Germany from 1933 to 1945, "the Third Reich".

WHAT IS NAZISM

Martin Broszat, described Nazism as 'the sinister embodiment of a dynamic nihilism devoid of ideological commitment'. He reached this conclusion because:

> The ideas of Nazism amounted to an irrational rag-bag of phobias, emotions, and illusions. All the ideas had been found in the pre-First World War völkisch (ethnic-nationalist) movements in Germany and Austria, and could be found in parties other than the Nazi Party after the war. Ideas were simply subsumed in propaganda, serving as a façade for demagogery.

German historian, Eberhard Jäckel, subjected Hitler's writings and speeches, especially his book Mein Kampf, to detailed analysis. Despite the rambling style, Jäckel maintained that Hitler's ideas amounted to a distinctive ideology in the sense outlined above: that is, forming a self-contained and self-reinforcing world view with ideas (however repulsive) following from each other once the original (irrational) premises had been accepted. These ideas were:

> Human history is nothing but racial struggle in which the strong survive and the weak die out. Political forms, such as the state, are merely means to the end of ensuring this survival. The Jews are the lowest form of humanity and most inferior race. Through their insidiousness, they had nevertheless gained control over both capitalism and Bolshevism. This had to be eliminated. Germany's future as a world power depended upon 'living space' to be found in Russia. Russia was run by 'Jewish-Bolshevism'. To destroy Russia by war would, therefore, amount to destroying the key platform of Jewish power, acquiring living space at the same time, and thereby ensuring Germany's future dominance. The road to this end was: nationalise the masses; gain power over the state; destroy internal enemies; build up defences; expand 'through the sword'.

Other leading Nazis, such as the Strasser brothers (Gregor and Otto), preferred an emphasis on a radical anti-capitalist social policy aimed at winning over workers. Others, for instance, Walther Darré, the agricultural guru of the party, wanted a 'back to the land' programme to safeguard Germany's peasantry. So Hitler's world-view and Nazi ideology overlapped, but were not identical. In a broader sense. Crucially Nazi ideology could be said to have consisted of the following dominant features: The central notion that sovereignty resided in the Volk—the ethnically defined 'people', or nation. The idea of a 'national community' (Volksgemeinschaft) in which a sense of ethnic unity would transcend and overcome all class and social divisions. Militant anti-Marxism, aimed not at defeating, but at destroying the main internal enemy. Unquestioned obedience to the Leader, whose authority came not from rank or status, but from his 'heroic achievements'. Extreme chauvinism and glorification of militarism and war. The primacy of the German nation over all else, and the superiority of Germany over all other nations.

During Nazism's rise to power, the broad message that the 'decadent' and divided democracy and the 'rotten' vestiges of the past would be ruthlessly swept away, that German rebirth would be brought about, and that Germany's internal enemies would be ruthlessly destroyed was what counted. The notion that Marxism would be eliminated, and that a strong and united 'national community' would be created were Hitler's two main propaganda lines, which he relentlessly and repeatedly drove home. Though a fixated ideologue, Hitler was also a masterly propagandist who knew that narrow ideas would not win the masses. So his message played to what would go down best and gain maximum support. Moreover, his ideas, though firmly held, were vaguely couched so that they could subsume most of the differing views of other party ideologues within them. Because Hitler was so indispensable to the Party as its main drawing-card, he was able to secure a leadership position which put him, in effect, over the Party and gradually meant that he became over time synonymous with the 'idea' of Nazism itself. His ideas came, accordingly, to dominate while any in conflict were ruled out.

Over the next years, those seeking to implement the vision that Hitler stood for—meaning removal of the Jews, and re-arming and rebuilding the nation to be ready for a future quest for dominance of Europe—drove along policy in numerous ways which were in accord with Hitler's ideological aims.

ORIGINS OF THE NAZI IDEOLOGY

The National Socialist ideology contained several basic points: Anti-Semitism, nationalism, militarism, and anti-communism. Jews were racially alien to Europe and were supposed to be the source of all European troubles, especially Communists. Second, Germany should become the strongest country in Europe because Germans were racially superior to other Europeans and should lead everyone else, even against their will. Third, force was seen as the bottom line in all of nature and in human life. As such, the military spirit was the truest expression of human creativity, courage, self-sacrifice, and survival. Finally, Russian bolshevism threatened European civilization and should be destroyed sooner or later.

National Socialism developed after 1918 as a counter-movement to the Bolshevik revolution and the democratic parliamentary system. Its intellectual roots were haphazard and to some extent even tangled: Nietzsche's "will to power," the racial theories of Gobineau and Houston Chamberlain, the "faith in destiny" of Richard Wagner, Mendel's theory of heredity, Haushofer's "geo-politics," or the social-Darwinist conceptions of Alfred Ploetz (1860–1940) were as much a part of the National Socialist ideology as the thought of Machiavelli, Fichte, Treitschke or Spengler.

As an ideology, Nazism (or National Socialism) is difficult to characterise because of its complexity and its fundamental lack of logical content. It builds on artificially created enemy figures. Four elements are characteristic of Nazism: it is an anti-ideology that builds more on criticism than suggestions for improvement; it is an anti-Semitic ideology, where the Jews (in an absurd combination with communism) are used as an explanation for all kinds of problems; it is a racist ideology that builds on a fundamental idea of the superiority of the Aryan (German) race; and it is, finally, an aggressively nationalistic ideology that puts the nation over the individual.

The Nazi, or National Socialist, ideology provided the goals and purposes for the Nazi regime. The expansion of living space, or lebensraum, and the elimination of the Jews are examples of Nazi ideology and what they wanted to accomplish once in power. Nazi ideology was everything to Adolf Hitler and his subordinates. They pounded their ideas into everything and everyone in German society. In other words, everything the Nazis did had a purpose and that purpose was to fulfill their detailed ideology. Unbeknownst to most, a German man named Arthur Moeller created the majority of National Socialist ideology before the Nazis gained power. Moeller was born in 1876 in the Rhineland and grew up opposed to the "imperialist" Germany and a critic of the Reich that helped cause World War I. After spending ten years as an expatriate where he developed his own ideas of an ideal Germany, he returned to his homeland after WWI to become the leading figure of the conservative revolution that was appealing many young men and ex-soldiers.

After publishing a newspaper promoting the new ideas with his colleagues, he wrote his influential Des Dritte Reich, in 1922. This book provided the Third Reich with its name and was deemed "a truly political religion". Moeller advocated the rejection of Marxism, liberalism, and any type of party or parliamentary government. He also rejected the West because of Versailles, its democratic institutions, and its capitalistic economy. In his country, he rejected the Weimar government because it was democratic and it was, as he believed, much too weak. In its place, Moeller believed Germany needed a strong dictator not to just rebuild Germany internally, but to implement a strong foreign policy platform to rebuild Germany's strength abroad. He believed the essence of politics was foreign policy, and in this case Moeller created a "socialist" foreign policy; defined as rectifying social grievances at home by punishing exploiters abroad. And, he believed, only a dictator was strong enough to implement this idea. As stated before, Moeller and his book had a huge influence on the Third Reich, but, more importantly, it gave National Socialists a direction before Hitler's ascension and a blueprint for the early party members to follow.

When Moeller's ideas finally started to be implemented in 1929, the Nazis started to gain power. During this year, the Weimar government fell and the Nazis made an impressive electoral showing in the elections. Only four years later, Hitler would become Chancellor and the other half of Nazi ideology would be implemented. And it was Adolf Hitler who created this other half of Nazi ideology. His ideas combined with Moeller's existing ideas created the overall Nazi ideology, or weltanschauung, that would become the platform and goals for the Nazi regime. It is also important to note here that this complete ideology is written down in detail, in Hitler's own hands, in Mein Kampf.

Hitler's own views were an extension of Moeller's; although Hitler had very practical ideas for his three main ideas for his new Germany: lebensraum, the elimination of the Jews, and the restoration of a traditional German society, or volksgeimenschaft. Hitler had similar views as Moeller with respect to lebensraum. He wanted to prove Germany's strength abroad and was convinced that Germany needed more land for its coming rise to power. Hitler created a master plan to expand Germany's territory. Hitler's first ideas of eliminating the Jews in the early 1920's meant emigration or deportation. This soon proved insufficient and he advocated the ideas of the concentration camps. This would become the infamous hallmark of the Nazi regime. It is important to note here that Hitler's plan for the elimination of the Jews must not be underestimated. When Hitler could have used every soldier and every piece of equipment for his Russian invasion in 1942, trains were still rolling across Germany on schedule allocating vast resources and soldiers to make sure Hitler's plan of extermination was not interrupted.

Hitler's final idea correlates with the elimination of the Jews. Hilter wanted to restore traditional German society. This was to be done by infusing the party's thoughts and ideology into the brains of the German society. The society would become hard-working Germans again, they would self-sacrifice for the greater good of a better Germany, but most importantly, they would become conscious of race and blood among Germans. Germany needed to be "cleansed" of all unwanted elements to create a master Aryan race. This entailed exterminating all Jews and any other "racially impure" citizens and creating laws forbidding intermarriage. On a more radical basis, the Nazis created laws for the sterilization of "mentally deficient" children so the "undesirable elements" would be prevented form "breeding", and Hitler, once the war started, even initiated an euthanasia program, or the mercy-killing of these "undesirable elements."

The overall Nazi ideology consisted of numerous elements. In the early years before the Nazis were actually in power, Arthur Moeller defined which direction the young National Socialists should go. Once Adolf Hilter came into power, he implemented his ideas for the Germany to become strong and powerful again by expanding their boundaries and creating a master, Aryan race. With this, Hitler writes in Mein Kampf, a powerful "Germanic State of the Germanic Nation" would be created.

Besides this we always find two great catchwords, 'Freedom' and 'Democracy,' used, I might say, as signboards. 'Freedom': under that term is understood, at least amongst those in authority who in fact carry on the Government, the possibility of an unchecked plundering of the masses of the people to which no resistance can be offered. The masses themselves naturally believe that under the term 'freedom' they possess the right to a quite peculiar freedom of motion—freedom to move the tongue and to say what they choose, freedom to move about the streets, etc. A bitter deception!

And the same is true of democracy. In general even in the early days both England and France had already been bound with the fetters of slavery. With, I might say, a brazen security these States are fettered with Jewish chains. . . .

Adolf Hitler, 28th April 1922. Munich

Chapter Two

History of Nazis

The dictator Adolf Hitler rose to power as leader of a political party, the National Socialist German Workers' Party (Nationalsozialistische Deutsche Arbeiterpartei or NSDAP for short). Germany during this period is also referred to as Nazi Germany. Nazism was also called National Socialism (German Nationalsozialismus). Adherents of Nazism were called Nazis. Nazism has been outlawed in modern Germany, although tiny remnants, known as Neo-Nazis, continue to operate in Germany and abroad. Some historical revisionists disseminate propaganda which denies or minimizes the Holocaust and other Nazi acts, and attempts to put a positive spin on the policies of the Nazi regime and the events which occurred under it.

The Nazi regime's nature as an extreme counter-revolutionary dictatorship can be traced back to the party's early days as a group during the revolutionary and counter-revolutionary upheavals that characterised the period immediately following Germany's defeat in World War I. In Bavaria itself, the Räterepublik was one of the more successful communist revolutionary attempts, eventually crushed with the help of Weimar government forces working with right wing Freikorps militia forces lead to the establishment of a counter-revolutionary government, which supported various right wing groups.(1) In this atmosphere of the völkisch right, it is little wonder that the Nazi party, and it's then rising star, Adolf Hitler, were so heavily influenced by their combined experiences in Munich at the time, as well as the trauma of defeat in the war. The völkisch politics of Munich and Bavaria were only one facet of the emerging Nazi ideology and style. From the Freikorps emerged the idea of the Sturmabteilung, more commonly known as the SA.(2) This paramilitary wing of the NSDAP party was to later play a violent role in the forming of the counter-revolutionary Nazi dictatorship. Understanding the origins of the Nazi party, and it's formulation as an anti-communist party is key to seeing how it became a counter-revolutionary dictatorship. A glance over the program of the NSDAP reveals little about the ideal to smash Bolshevism yet encourages the promotion of Germans and German interests above all others.(3)

The Nazi Party was formed as the German Workers party by Anton Drexler, Dietrich Eckhart and Gottfried Feder in 1919. Drexler, who was the original leader of the party, had strong nationalistic views and was Anti-Semitic. This small political party was noted by the armed forces as being a potential Socialist threat and a spy, Adolf Hitler, was sent to investigate the party to assess how much of a threat the party was. Hitler became fascinated with the politics of the group, and began an active participation in the activities of the German Workers Party. This led to him rapidly becoming the member of the GWP executive responsible for propaganda and in turn his skills as a public speaker led to him becoming the mouthpiece of the movement.*

His skills as a political speaker and his assertive manner within party meetings soon led to Hitler becoming the recognised leader of the party. It was he who then began to formulate policies. This culminated in the production, in 1920, of a 25 point programme or manifesto. This outlined the aims of the NSDAP (The Party name had by now been changed from 'German Workers party'). The programme, along with Hitler's speeches, illustrates what the ideology of the party was in its early days and, via speeches, how these ideals and aims might be put into practice. The programme is a curious mixture of ideas ranging from demands for the Unification of Germany through to the expulsion of Jews from the German nation. Economic ideals are noted also in the programme: Nationalisation of corporations, land reform and welfare policies are all suggested. Thus a basis was in place from which the party could sell its programme to a wide audience.

In 1923 Hitler and his party found Bavaria, where they were based, in a state of chaos. Along with other right wing groups the Nazi's sensed the opportunity to take control and begin the National Socialist Revolution. This led to the Munich Putsch, which though a failure, propelled Hitler into the National arena as his trial was widely publicised and the relatively lenient sentence he received had a consequence of breaking a coalition government (Socialists withdrew from the coalition led by Stresemann, resulting in a new coalition being formed). Hitler used his imprisonment to rethink the strategy of the NSDAP. Whilst serving his sentence he wrote the first edition of Mein Kampf, "My Struggle". This book outlined the history of Hitler's political development and in the section section of the book goes on to discuss political ideology and the way forward.

Whilst imprisoned HItler made several decisions that would radically alter the way forward for the Nazi Party. He realised that a revolution of the kind attempted in Munich was unlikely to succeed. Therefore his revolution would have to be a legal one, via the democratic process. This decision changes the manner in which the Nazi Party must organise itself, and the way in which it sells its ideas. From this point onwards, there is a clear attempt at a broader sectoral appeal, with the Nazi propaganda machine becoming increasingly significant. Hitler knew that he had to convince the masses that National Socialism was right for them—and his time in prison allowed him the time to plan for this.

Hitler's 'Mein Kampf' (My Struggle), which was a cross between his autobiography and a list of his political ideas:

- The German people were a master race, a 'Herrenvolk'. All other races (Slavs, Jews, black people and gypsies) were inferior 'Untermenschen'.
- Germany should be re-united and seize land to the east, 'Lebensraum'.
- To make Germany great again, a new leader was needed. Democracy was a weak system and should be replaced by dictatorship. Communism should be destroyed.
- German citizens should be prepared to subordinate themselves to the needs of the state.
- Men and women had separate roles in society, which they had to be prepared for from the earliest age.

WHY DID SUPPORT FOR NAZIS INCREASE?

In 1928 the Nazis won support outside of Bavaria for virtually the first time. They began to win votes in farming areas of north Germany, as prices fell. But their big break came in 1929.

On 3 October 1929 Gustav Stresemann died. He had been responsible, more than any other politician, for Germany's recovery in the 1920s. On 24 October 1929 Wall Street, the American Stock Exchange crashed. US bankers called in their loans to Germany. German companies had to close down. This led to the Depression of the 1930s, which affected Germany more than any other country. By 1932 6,000,000 Germans (one in three of all workers) were out of work. Unemployment pay only lasted six months. After that came real poverty and homelessness. The Weimar government seemed unable to deal with the crisis (along with most governments in the world). The Social Democrats refused to cut unemployment pay and so went into opposition. As they were the largest single party this made it difficult to make coalitions.

Governments came and went. Support for Weimar, never strong, declined and people began to look for other solutions to Germany's problems. In this situation, President Hindenburg began to allow Chancellor Bruning to use his emergency powers on a regular basis to by-pass the Reichstag. Democracy in Germany had really ended by 1932. From 1929 support for the Nazis rose steadily.

1928   12 members of the Reichstag
1930   107 members
1932   230 members

WHY DID SUPPORT FOR THE HITLER AND THE NAZIS GO UP SO QUICKLY?

Hitler told the German people that the problems of the Depression were not their fault. He blamed the Jews and the Weimar democrats for Germany's problems. He used them as a scapegoat. The Nazi Party propaganda chief, Goebbels, had Hugenberg's money and newspapers to back them. Hitler hired a private plane to fly around Germany. He was the first politician to do this. Goebbels organised torchlight processions, rallies, radio broadcasts, films. Nazi propaganda was far ahead of any of their rivals. Hitler said that he would be able to solve the problems. He offered strong leadership and easy solutions.

Hitler said that he would do away with the Treaty of Versailles, which had treated Germany so badly and make their country great again. He was always backed up by large numbers of disciplined and uniformed followers. The SA rose in numbers from 30,000 in 1929 to 440,000 in 1932. The discipline, the processions and the uniforms gave the impression of toughness and knowing what was needed. It reminded people of the old days under the Kaiser. The violence of the SA increased. This gave the impression of action and purpose. They particularly attacked Communists, which pleased middle class and business people. It also made the Weimar system look as though they couldn't keep order. Hitler promised different things to different groups of people. To businessmen he promised that he would control the Trade Unions and deal with the Communists. To workers he promised that he would provide jobs.

HITLER BECOMES CHANCELLOR

As the situation in Germany became more and more desperate, people were more and more ready to listen to the ideas of Hitler. In 1932 Hitler stood in the presidential elections against Hindenburg. Hindenburg won 17 million votes, Hitler won 11 million. In the July 1932 general election the Nazis became the biggest party in Reichstag, but Hindenburg refused to appoint Hitler Chancellor. Franz von Papen became Chancellor. In the November 1932 the Nazis lost some support, but were still the biggest party in the Reichstag. Franz von Papen was replaced as chancellor by General Kurt von Schleicher. Von Papen was furious that von Schleicher had taken his place and was determined to get rid of him. In January 1933.he suggested that Hindenburg appoint Hitler as chancellor, with von Papen as Vice-Chancellor in a coalition government. Von Papen thought he could control Hitler. Hindenburg against his better judgement agreed. On 30 January 1933 Hitler became chancellor of Germany.

Yet the party program was not exclusively adhered to, as when the Nazi party finally obtained power through electorial "success" (they did not win a majority of the vote, yet their high percentage, 33% by the time of Hitler's appointment to Chancellor, made them the largest party in the Reichstag) it was the combination of the violent attacks of the SA on the opposition to the regime, for the most part communists, though other political creeds and minority groups were caught up, and the use of the Reichstag Fire Decree of February 1933, that gave the Nazi party control over Germany. (4) Counter-revolution had been a part of German politics since the war, and Hitler and the Nazi's took it to new extremes. The Reichstag Fire and the following "Law against the New Formulation of Parties in July 1933, gave the Nazi's the legal grip on power, and it was left to the SA, the Gestapo, and Hitler's personal body guard, the SS, to enforce that power.

WHO SUPPORTED HITLER?

During his campaigns Hitler had offered different things to different people. The middle classes supported him because he offered stability and protection from communism. At first many working men supported Hitler, because he offered work and security. He claimed that the real strength of Germany lay in its workers. Many women supported Hitler, because he seemed to offer a better family life. However his greatest support came from children, who seemed to have admired the order and discipline of the Nazi movement and to whom Hitler set out to make a special appeal. Opposed to Hitler were the communists and socialists, they saw that his ideas would take away basic freedoms. Members of some churches, especially the German Lutheran Church opposed him. However, Hitler claimed to be a Roman Catholic and this led some Catholics to back him at first.

EDUCATION AND IDEOLOGY

The whole function of education was to create good Nazis. From 1935–8 the membership of the HJ grew from 3.5m to 7.7m Young children were education physically, intellectually and morally within the spirit of Socialism. The HJ were the future of the Volksgemeinschaft and very much the hotbed of the future Master Race. Successful candidates and graduates were guaranteed officer training and the SS. For most there was the sense of belonging, unity and nationhood. They were provided with physical recreation, activity, respect within the new Nazi state, 3 Reichsmarks a day, food, uniforms and an adventurous life.

In essence, though, the HJ was a local movement with national pretensions. It was the Nazi state instrument to run its ideological training programs, youth leadership education and at every level there was a sense of competition. As such the Nazi state along with the HJ stunted creativity, imagination and individual vision. Some schools were definitely infiltrated by Nazis and Nazi ideology. Others were not so targeted. Subjects included war, biology, race and physical education—the subjects deemed acceptable to the Nazi authorities who pursued headmasters and screened teachers aggressively. Many teachers lamented the reduction in curriculum subjects and to the surrounding of the next generation within an environment of brutality and mathematics. Even so, it was hard to get away from the issues of war preparation and racial hatred. It was an active movement to reduce academic standards in education, in place of simplified and bite sized portions. This was a deliberate policy of stunting creativity and reducing the chances of the average German forming any opposition to the Nazi policy. Additionally, education was no longer seemed as the avenue of intellectualism and scholastic achievement. It was now seen as hanging outside the boundaries of decency and the pursuit of individualism.

As such, education was the primary function of training the nation to serve the economic and military needs of the nation and the Volk. Education was primarily physical for the boys and domestic education for the girls. This would fit in with Nazi ideological plans for the different sexes and their places in the future Germany.Textbooks and other education materials were also doctored and manipulated to reflect Nazi plans. Race, physical training, history, biology and the Jews was the first to be revised.

CREATION OF THE TOTALITARIAN STATE:
THE ELIMINATION OF OPPOSITION

Von Papen's hopes of controlling Hitler were short-lived. Hitler immediately called for a general election on 5 March and was determined to gain the overall majority that he needed to make himself dictator legally. A week before the elections the Reichstag building was set on fire. The Nazis, (who have sometimes been accused of starting the fire themselves), blame the Communists. 4,000 Communists were arrested. In March 1933, before the election, Goering, the Minister for the Interior in Prussia, enrolled SA members as special constables. Other parties were attacked and arrested. In the election the Nazis win 17.3 million votes, 233 seats, the biggest party, but still not a majority in Reichstag. 22 million vote for other parties. But with the support of Hugenberg's National Party the Nazis now controlled the Reichstag. When it met on 17 March, the Socialists and Communists stayed away. Hitler could now do as he liked.

On 23 March the Reichstag passed the Enabling Act, 1933. This gave Hitler the power to by-pass the Reichstag and make laws without its consent for four years. It was passed with the help of the Nationalists and with the Reichstag building surrounded by armed SA members. Local government was taken over by the Nazis; each of the 18 provinces was given a Nazi governor, April, 1933. Local parliaments were abolished. Only Nazis could become civil servants, judges. Trade unions were abolished in May 1933. All other parties were banned, July 1933. Their leaders were arrested, or fled abroad. The first concentration camp, at Dachau, was set up for political opponents in 1933. 1934 Hindenburg died. Hitler becomes President and Chancellor combined, calling himself simply, The Leader—Der Fuhrer. The army swore its oath of loyalty to Hitler, personally.

THE NIGHT OF THE LONG KNIVE

Once Hitler became Chancellor, he began to face opposition within the Nazi Party. Hitler's only rival was Ernst Rohm, head of the SA, 3 million strong by 1934. They were more socialist than Hitler, more working class and eager for power. Roehm wanted a socialist revolution in Germany and also wanted the SA to become units in the German Army, with him at the head. This would make him more powerful than Hitler.

Hitler did not want the socialists within the party to take control. He wanted a right wing dictatorship. He needed the support of the army for his plans for war and knew that the generals would not accept Roehm as their leader. Hitler had to act before President Hindenburg died. It would be very difficult to deny Roehm power when Hitler became Fuhrer. Roehm claimed that the SA was growing rapidly. He put the membership at 3,000,000, although it was probably nearer 500,000. Roehm ordered all members of the SA to go on holiday for the month of July 1934 and summoned the leaders to

Munich for a conference. On the night of 30 June 1934, 400 SA leaders, including Rohm, were assassinated by the SS on Hitler's orders. Also murdered was General Kurt von Schleicher and his wife.

THE NAZI STATE: PROPAGANDA, EDUCATION, YOUTH MOVEMENTS, THE ARTS, SPORT, ENTERTAINMENT AND RELIGION

The Gestapo (Geheime Staats Polizei), or secret police, was set up and was run by Himmler after 1936. People were arrested and imprisoned without trial. Evidence from informers was used—people were encouraged to inform on neighbours, colleagues, even their own family. Every block or street had an informer who reported on any behaviour that might suggest non-Nazi views e.g. not giving the Hitler salute. Nazi "People's Courts" tried people, often in secret. In 1934 the 'Burning of the books' took place. Nazi students took books by Jewish or anti-Nazi authors out of libraries and burnt them in huge bonfires. Goebbels controlled all forms of communication: books, newspapers, films, newsreels, radio as well as music and the arts. No non-Nazi views were ever heard. Only messages praising Hitler and the Nazis reached the public. Cheap radios were made. Hitler's portrait was in every public place. People almost worshipped him; he was portrayed as Germany's saviour from disaster. This total control of every aspect of life and attempt to keep even people's thoughts under control is called totalitarianism.

Children joined at the age of five and stayed until eighteen. Membership was virtually compulsory. Boys joined the Pimpfen, then the German Youth and then the Hitler Youth. Girls joined the League of German Maidens. Children took part in 'fun' activities, camping, sports and outings. These helped make the Youth movements popular at first. They also had lectures about Nazi ideas, like racism. The girls were taught about child-rearing. The boys did activities which prepared them for the army: cleaning rifles, reading maps, throwing hand grenades, doing mock parachute jumps, going on long marches. The meetings were in the evenings and at weekends. Girls found that they had little time for homework. This was to prevent them having a career. Children were encouraged to spy on their parents and report what they did and said. In 1933 30% of young people in Germany were in the Nazi Youth movements; by 1938 it was 82%. In 1939 it became compulsory.

By the later 1930s some young people were getting resentful of the time it took up, the boring lectures they had all heard before at school, the incomprehensible readings from Mein Kampf.

NUREMBERG LAWS

From 1933 Jews were subjected to increasing persecution in Nazi Germany. At first they were banned from some professions, doctors, dentists, the civil service, for example. Nazis also called for Jewish shops to be boycotted. Then in 1935 the Nuremberg Laws were announced; these made Jews second class citizens and prevented them from marrying non-Jews. All kinds of civil rights were removed: voting, going to university, travelling, attending a theatre, cinema or sporting event. In 1938 a young Jew assassinated a German diplomat in France. This led to an organised attack on Jewish shops, houses and synagogues all over Germany. 91 Jews killed; 20,000 arrested. The Jewish community in Germany had to pay a "fine" of 1 billion marks. This was known as Kristallnacht (the night of broken glass). From early 1939 Jews were banned from owning businesses; all men to add the name 'Israel' and all women the name 'Sara' to their own. The aim of the Nazis was to force Jews to leave Germany and many did, going to Britain, France and the USA in particular. But once war broke out this became more difficult, so Jews were forced into Concentration Camps.

OPPOSITION TO THE NAZIS WITHIN GERMANY

There were three main groups of people who tried to oppose the Nazis. Political parties like the Communists and the Socialists. They were banned from 1933, but worked underground in secret, keeping their organisation together and publishing newsletters. There was a big communist group called the Red Orchestra, which became very important during the Second World War. Young People. There were a number of student groups who distributed leaflets and organised meetings. One group, at Munich University, called the White Rose, centred around Hans and Sophie Scholl. They were arrested and executed in 1944. Some young people simply rejected the Nazis. 'Swing' groups listened to American jazz and openly admired American fashions. 'Edelweiss Pirates' were working class Groups who mocked the self-righteous Nazis and refused to join the Hitler Youth. Religious groups. These were the most difficult to deal with as many Germans would not have accepted attacks on the Catholic and Protestant Churches. Some Christians spoke out against the Nazis, like Martin Niemoller and Dietrich Bonhoeffer. Later, in the war years, some people in the army became horrified by the Nazis' brutality and worried that Hitler was leading Germany to certain defeat. In 1944 some officers planted a bomb in his war-room, but it failed to kill him. 5,000 people were executed in retaliation.

Terror was a very important factor. Everybody knew that they were being watched. In every block of flats there was someone recording when people went in and out and who they met. People could be arrested at any moment and never be seen again. Children spied on their parents. Hitler tried to break down the family and make children loyal to him. He was described as their father in schoolbooks. Endless and powerful propaganda had its effect. It was impossible to get anti-Nazi views heard at all and the mass of people only heard good things. There was no mass feeling of resentment against Hitler, at least until the middle of the war. The social impact of Nazism on social classes: the role and status of women: employment opportunities in the economy.

THE EFFECTS OF NAZI RULE ON THE LIVES OF MEN AND WOMEN

The Nazi Party was a man's party. There were no women in senior positions. Hitler and the Nazis did not believe in equality for the sexes. Women had to stay at home, produce more children and look after the family. This was for both racial reasons, to produce more racially-pure Germans, and economic reasons, to solve unemployment by removing women from the labour market. There was a lot of propaganda about the ideal German family. Photographs and posters showed the woman looking after the children and the man going out to work and protecting the wife. Women were forced to give up work when they got married. They could not be civil servants, lawyers, judges or doctors. Men were to be preferred to women in job applications. Couples received a loan of 1,000 marks on getting married. Less and less of this loan had to be paid back the more children you had. Women with hereditary diseases or metal illness were sterilised so as to keep the German race 'pure'. Unmarried women could volunteer to have a child by a 'pure Aryan' SS member.

Nazi propaganda discouraged wearing make-up, high heels, perfume, smoking in public. Women's roles can be summarised as three 'Ks' Kinder, Kirche, Kuche, children, church, cooking (or kitchen). But most people found themselves getting better off; transport improved, there was more security. Germany seemed to be recovering. In 1936 the Olympic Games were held in Berlin and the Rhineland was reoccupied. Both these events made Germans proud of their country. Workers had few rights. Trade unions were abolished and they had to join the Labour Front. Wages were low and rose much more slowly than business profits. Conditions of work in the Labour Front were tough, but it was at least a job. The 'Strength Through Joy' campaign gave workers cheap holidays, concerts, sport. The attempt to build a cheap car, the Volkswagen, failed until after the war. After what had happened to their country in the years after 1919 and during the Depression, many people were prepared to accept Nazism. They preferred to close their eyes to the arrests of opponents, the mistreatment of the Jews, the Nazi corruption. At least until the war started going badly, about 1942, most people were quite ready to go along with the Nazis.

ECONOMIC POLICIES AND REARMAMENT

Before the Nazis came to power the National Labour Service had been started. This used government money to provide jobs for the unemployed, building bridges, roads and forests. The Nazis took up and expanded these schemes. Hitler was especially keen on the building of the first motorways, the Autobahns. All men had to spend six months in the Labour Service. They only earnt about 50p a week, wore uniforms and marched like soldiers. Much of the work was done by hand and not by machinery. This meant that there were more jobs.

German re-armament gave a huge boost to industry, which soon had millions of new jobs. At first secretly, then quite openly, Hitler ordered the building of submarines, aircraft and tanks. This was quite contrary to the terms of the Treaty of Versailles. The army was increased from 100,000 to 1,400,000 by 1939. Many people were removed from the list of unemployed, for example Jews, many women and the young men in the National Labour Front. By 1936 recorded unemployment was down from 6 million to 1 million; by 1938 industry was short of workers and during the Second World War workers were forced into German factories from all the countries the Nazis had overrun. Hitler wanted the German economy to be self-sufficient so that it would be able to operate even in a war. Foreign imports were restricted and research put into finding substitutes for rubber, petrol, coffee and cotton. This policy was known as Autarky.

HITLER'S LEGAL RISE TO POWER

The National Socialist German Workers Party (NSDAP or Nazi) was perhaps the most counter revolutionary dictatorship that history has ever born witness to. From the twisted ideological world of the demagogue Adolf Hitler; to its extreme implementation by such notorious figures as Reinhard Heydrich and Heinrich Himmler, the Nazi dictatorship which ruled Germany from 1933, then progressively Europe from 1938 onwards, proved itself to be a horrifying lesson in how far counter revolution could be taken, and the nightmares it could turn into reality. From a dictatorship based on terrorising the left and using a mixture of coercion and legitimacy to gain power, Hitler, the ideological drive of the regime, would finally turn his gaze eastwards in 1941, and unleash the most massive counter revolutionary war that the world has ever seen.

To examine the extent of counter-revolution as a major facet of Nazi ideology, one must only look to how counter-revolution evolved itself into the "crusade" against Bolshevism, Operation Barbarossa. The massive invasion of Russia was the culmination of counter-revolutionary ideas, voiced in the form of a Jewish-Bolshevik conspiracy in Hitler's work Mein Kampf. However, it was the implementation of counter-revolution within the Soviet Union that showed the true extent of the counter-revolutionary facets to Adolf Hitler's ideology. The use of the SS Sonderkommando (not to be confused with the Jewish concentration camp guards) in rear area actions during the Barbarossa campaign underlined the idea of it being a show down between Nazism and Communism. The order that allowed the Sonderkommando to operate in conjunction with advanced Wehrmacht forces was justified by Field Marshall Keitel, a leading Nazi supporter within the Heer; . . . that the downfall of 1918, the German people's period of suffering which followed and the struggle against National Socialism—with the many blood sacrifices endured by the movement—can be traced to Bolshevik influence. No German should forget this. (5)

Yet Keitel's order for the Wehrmacht to ignore the rules of war in the East were further suplemented when Himmler informed selected SS leaders that a population reduction of some 30 million Slavs would be required in the east.6 If these two statements, both from powerful figures within the regime were not enough, General Jodl, Chief of Operations staff in Wehrmacht High Command (OKW), provided perhaps the starkest show of counter-revolutionary drive within Nazi Germany, excluding Hitler himself, ". . . all Bolshevist leaders or commissars must be liquidated forthwidth."(6)

Far earlier than Barbarossa, the Nazi regime's counter-revolutionary activities were put into action in Spain by the involvement of German forces in supporting General Franco in the Spainish civil war. To Hitler, involvement in Spain was crucial for halting any jewish-bolshevik threat to the Reich and Spain was essentially where the line would be drawn in the sand.(7) Yet it was Poland where the Sonderkommando/Einsatzgruppen would first be unleashed, and this merely played itself out as a form of brutalising the local population into submission.(8) Yet the imperialist aims of Hitler's Reich over Poland were part of the counter-revolutionary drive of Hitler's ideology, and the conquering of Poland was a step towards a military counter-revolution in the Soviet Union which would both eradicate jewish-bolshevism, and provide the German people with the Lebensraum which Hitler believed the master race required.

Only in analysing the barbarity of the war in Russia, can one truly see the extent and the methods employed by the Nazi regime to reach their counter-revolutionary and racial goals. In the "Guidelines for the Treatment of Political Commissars" issued June 6, 1941, 18 days prior to the launching of Barbarossa contains the following examples of counter-revolution in preparation.

The army must be aware of the following:

1. In this battle it would be mistaken to show mercy or respect for international law towards such elements (political commissars). . . .
2. The barbaric, Asiatic fighting methods are originated by the political commissars. Action must therefore be taken against them immediately, without further consideration, and with all severity.(9)

The German counter-revolution was not to be carried out solely by the Sonderkommando, but local populations in the east were also encouraged to take out their anger against Jews and Communists.(10) Yet this was permissible only for a time, and only so long as the German's needed their help. As the Ostheer (Eastern Army) and the Sonderkommando with their assorted SS assistance, eventually local populations were being caught up, and as shown earlier, the plan was to starve off approximately 30 million "slavs" in the East. The SS in particular ran extensive recruiting campaigns in occupied Europe, these campaigns were based around a crusade of Europe against bolshevism, rather than Germany against bolshevism

The preoccupation of Waffen SS recruiting aimed at the anti-Bbolshevik crusade shows clearly how much this aspect of Nazi ideology mattered. If one was to try to divide the Nazi ideology into three key areas, they would be racial: social Darwinist ideas about Jews and subhuman races, nationalist: promotion of German culture, the ideal of a greater German Reich and the primacy of Germany as the master of Europe, and counter-revolution: anti-bolshevik counter-revolution tied in closely with the anti-Semite sentiments of the regime. The SS, both the Waffen SS and the various security organisations of the SS, most notoriously the Einsatzgruppen/Sonderkommando, were the key tools in this counter-revolutionary pillar of National Socialism. Yet the war against bolshevism was closely tied into the racial programs of the regime, and thus the genocide of the Jewish population in Europe was essentially the precussor to another genocide against the Slavs in the East. Furthermore the war in Poland had softened up the Wehrmacht to working with the SS for removing obstacles for occupation, in Poland this was the ruling class, but in Russia it was to be both Communists, Jews, and ultimately a large number of Russians.(12) License for this barbarism was given by Hitler in the early stages of planning for Barbarossa, yet he most clearly showed it in a speech on the 31st of March, 1941,

> Communism is an enormous danger for our future. We must forget the concept of comradeship between soldiers. A Communist is no comrade before or after the battle. This is a war of annihilation. If we do not grasp this, we shall still beat the enemy, but thirty years later we shall again have to fight the Communist foe. We do not wage war to preserve the enemy." (13)

The concept of a war of annihilation was key to how counter-revolutionary Nazi ideology was going to be brought into reality. Yet the SS alone could not bring this to fruition, and thus the Wehrmacht, and more over, the Ostheer was to be brought in to assist in the brutal plan to annihilate bolshevism. And while the Ostheer and the Heer in general were not Nazis, the hatred of bolshevism did indeed run deep in their ranks. For the main, the illegal Barbarossa orders were passed onto troops, only in a few cases did commanders refuse to pass the orders on. Yet many soldiers took a grotesque interest in the counter-revolutionary activities, and the 6th Army was forced to issue the following order in August 1941,

> In various places within the army's area of responsibility, organs of the SD, of the Reichsführer's SS and chiefs of the German Police have been carrying out necessary executions of criminal, bolshevik and mostly Jewish elements. There have been cases of off-duty soldiers volunteering to help the SD with their executions, or acting as spectators and taking photographs.(14)

The order went on to prohibit soldiers from the army participating in any such action unless directly ordered to. The level of counter-revolutionary fervour had spread far beyond the Nazi party itself and had begun to infest even the Wehrmacht itself.

The Nazi regime was clearly the most counter-revolutionary dictatorship that has existed. Its invasion of Russia, it's aim to annihilate bolshevism, has never been tried since. The sheer scale and size of it's attempts to uproot and destroy it's supposed Jewish-Bolshevik conspiracy go beyond the norms of war and diplomacy. The methods employed by the SS and in assistance to them, the Wehrmacht, demonstrate clearly the great extent to which counter-revolution had become not just part of the party and state, but also of social life. With communism having been largely defeated in Germany following the defeat in World War One, the Nazi counter-revolution merely crushed its remaining elements within Germany, and then sought to finish the job by invading Russia. Through the methods of genocide and occupation, the Nazis hoped that they could once and forever defeat bolshevism.

WHY THE NAZIS CAME TO POWER

Conditions

How the Nazis came into power in Germany is obviously an important question. A few reasons should be mentioned in this context:

- As early as before World War I, Germany had been a very complex society, characterised by equal parts old-fashioned feudalism and modern industrialisation.
- The country had a very strong tradition for militarism and loyalty towards the authorities.
- In connection with the war effort during World War I, the German population had been impressed with a strong nationalism by the imperial government, in order to facilitate internal control and international aggression.
- Biological-racial ideas of the superiority of the Aryan race were widely respected as a legitimate point of view.
- In the years following World War I, Germany was under enormous national "stress" because of the military defeat and the subsequent economic ruin.

Nazism presented the German population with an easy explanation to all their problems: Jews and democracy. It was the "International Jewry" that had been responsible for Germany's defeat in World War I and the humiliating peace treaty. Democracy, i.e. the elected officials of the Weimar Republic, was responsible for the economic depression of the early 1930's. The Nazis cleverly played on the "political paranoia" of the middle class, and in this respect the Jews and communists worked excellently as representations of the enemy.

Chapter Three

Nazi Ideology

NSDAP'S PARTY PROGRAMME

The Nazi Party's political programme was formulated in 1920, and according to its wording it was 'inalterable'. It was never revised, but many of the ideological principles were never transformed into practical policy when the Nazis came into power. This was particularly the case for the party programme's economical principles, which were deemed much too socialistic. Among other things, the Nazi Party demanded the abolition of all trusts (§13), equal share of profits in all businesses (§14), and a prohibition against any kind of capital income (§11). Such ideas were of course completely unacceptable to the party's big business supporters, and they were never realised.

The party programme was characteristically filled with negative suggestions. This fits well with the fact that Nazism really was an anti-ideology: anti-democratic, anti-communist, anti-Semitic, anti-capitalistic, and anti-Western.

1. We demand the union of all Germans-on the basis of the right of self-determination of peoples-in a Greater Germany.
2. We demand equality of the German People with all other nations, the abrogation of the peace treaties of Versailles and Saint German.
3. We demand land and soil (colonies) for the nourishment of our people and for the settlement of our excess population.
4. Only he who is a folk comrade can be a citizen. Only he who is of German blood, regardless of his church, can be a folk comrade. No Jew, therefore, can be a folk comrade.
5. He who is not a citizen shall Live in Germany only as a guest and must be governed by laws for aliens.

6. The right to make decisions about leadership and law belongs only to citizens. We therefore demand that every public office, no matter what kind, whether national, state, or local, be staffed only by citizens. We oppose the corrupting parliamentary system of filling offices only according to the needs of the party and without regards for character or ability.
7. We demand that the state pledge itself to assure the productivity and livelihood of citizens above all others. If it is not possible to support the entire population, members of a foreign nation (non-citizen) are to be expelled.
8. Any further immigration of non-Germans is to be prevented. We demand that all non-Germans who have entered Germany since August 2, 1914, be forced to leave the Reich immediately.
9. All citizen must possess equal rights and duties.
10. It must be the primary duty of every citizen to work mentally or physically. The activities of the individual may not conflict with the interests of the general public must be carried on within the framework of the whole and for the good of all
11. The Common Good for all before the Individual Good.
25. In order to carry out these policies we demand: creation of a strong central authority in the Reich. The central parliament must have unlimited authority over the entire Reich and all its organizations. The formation of chambers according to occupation and profession, to carry out in the individual states the basic law enacted by the Reich.

The leaders of the party pledge that they will relentlessly seek the implementation of these points, if necessary at the cost of their lives. 15

HITLER AND MEIN KAMPF

The most coherent effort at presenting the ideological characteristics of Nazism can be found in Hitler's autobiographical work, Mein Kampf ('My Struggle'). This book was written between 1923 and 1924, while Hitler was in prison for participating in the famous (and failed) Beer Hall Putsch in Munich. In his book, Hitler presents his inalterable 'worldview' (German: Weltanschauung), which after the Nazi takeover became the political-ideological basis of the new regime.

Hitler's Weltanschauung was entirely a system of prejudices, which by no means were the result of any serious contemplation. Characteristically, Hitler's worldview included:

- A racist interpretation of world history, where the Aryan race is presented as 'creating cultures' and the Jewish race as 'destroying cultures'.
- A social-Darwinist view of life: the strong survive, the weak perish. This goes for man as well as for the rest of nature.
- A love of anything militaristic: only in war does man show his true abilities.
- A belief that Germany can (and should) become a world power.

Fundamental for all these aspects was Hitler's steady belief in the biological and cultural superiority of the Aryan race. It was consequently a very important part of Hitler's ideology that the races should not be mixed. He saw the 'purity of the blood' a prerequisite for the coming greatness of the German people.

Hitler's Mein Kampf

Hitler served only eight months of his five-year term. While in prison, he wrote the first volume of Mein Kampf (2ed part was written in 1927–1927). It was partly an autobiographical book (although filled with glorified inaccuracies, self-serving half-truths and outright revisionism) which also detailed his views on the future of the German people. There were several targets of the vicious diatribes in the book, such as democrats, Communists, and internationalists. But he reserved the brunt of his vituperation for the Jews, whom he portrayed as responsible for all of the problems and evils of the world, particularly democracy, Communism, and internationalism, as well as Germany's defeat in the War. Jews were the German nation's true enemy, he wrote. They had no culture of their own, he asserted, but perverted existing cultures such as Germany's with their parasitism. As such, they were not a race, but an anti-race:

> "[The Jews'] ultimate goal is the denaturalization, the promiscuous bastardization of other peoples, the lowering of the racial level of the highest peoples as well as the domination of his racial mishmash through the extirpation of the volkish intelligentsia and its replacement by the members of his own people,"

On the contrary, the German people were of the highest racial purity and those destined to be the master race according to Hitler. To maintain that purity, it was necessary to avoid intermarriage with subhuman races such as Jews and Slavs. . . . Germany could stop the Jews from conquering the world only by eliminating them. By doing so, Germany could also find Lebensraum, living space, without which the superior German culture would decay.

This living space, Hitler continued, would come from conquering Russia (which was under the control of Jewish Marxists, he believed) and the Slavic countries. This empire would be launched after democracy was eliminated and a "Führer" called upon to rebuild the German Reich." A second volume of Mein Kampf was published in 1927. It included a history of the Nazi party to that time and its program, as well as a primer on how to obtain and retain political power, how to use propaganda and terrorism, and how to build a political organization. While Mein Kampf was crudely written and filled with embarrassing tangents and ramblings, it struck a responsive chord among its target and those Germans who believed it was their destiny to dominate Europe. The book sold over five million copies by the start of World War II.

HITLER'S POLITICAL VIEWS

Hitler lived in Vienna for several years, working at odd jobs and absorbing the ideas of Austrian right-wing extremists. In 1913, he left Vienna and moved to Munich in southern Germany. He took with him the basic political ideas to which he would remain committed for the balance of his life. Central to Hitler's thought were his notions of race. He believed in the racial superiority of the Germanic peoples (the Aryan race) and in the inferiority of other races, especially Jews but also Slavs and blacks. Hitler also advocated the Pan-German ideology that was popular among many Austrian extremists. Pan-Germanism held the view that all Germans should be united in a single state. In addition, Hitler was hostile to the ideology of Marxism, which emphasized the unity of the international working class rather than racial solidarity.

The following extracts illustrate some of the political ideas of Adolf Hitler (1889–1945):

> In that we deny the principle of parliamentary democracy we strike the strongest blow for the right of the nation to the self-determination of its own life. For in the parliamentary system we see no genuine expression of the nation's will—a will which cannot logically be anything else than a will to the maintenance of the nation—but we do see a distortion, if not a perversion, of that will. The will of a nation to the self-determination of its being manifests itself most clearly and is of most use when its most capable minds are brought forth. They form the representative leaders of a nation, they alone can be the pride of a nation—certainly never the parliamentary politician who is the product of the ballot box and thinks only in terms of votes. The constructive development of the future leadership of the nation through its most able men will take years; the intelligent education of the German people will take decades.[16]

Internationalism is weakness in the life of nations. What is there that is born of internationalism? Nothing. The real values of human culture were not born of internationalism, but they were created by the whole heritage and tradition of the people [das Volkstum]. When peoples no longer possess creative power they become international. Wherever there is weakness in regard to spiritual matters in the life of nations, internationalism makes its appearance. It is no coincidence that a people, namely the Jews, which does not have any real creative ability, is the carrier of this internationalism. It is the people with the least creative power and talent. It dominates only in the field of crooked and speculative economy. . . . The Jew, as a race, has a remarkable instinct of self-preservation, but as an individual he has no cultural abilities at all. He is the demon of the disintegration of nations — the symbol of continual destruction of peoples. If the first of May, therefore, is to have any meaning in the life of peoples, it can be only a glorification of the national, creative idea as against the international idea of decay. [17]

I do not want even to speak of the Jews. They are simply our old enemies, their plans have suffered shipwreck through us, and they rightly hate us, just as we hate them. We realize that this war can end only either in the Wiping out of the Germanic nations, or by the disappearance of Jewry from Europe. On September 3rd I spoke in the Reichstag — and I dislike premature prophecies — and I said that this war would not end the way the Jews imagine, that is, in the extinction of the European Aryan nations, but that the result of this war would be the destruction of Jewry. For the first time, it will not be the others who will bleed to death, but for the first time the genuine ancient Jewish law, "an eye for an eye, a tooth for a tooth," is being applied. The more this struggle spreads, the more anti Semitism will spread — and world Jewry may rely on this. It will find nourishment in every prison camp, it will find nourishment in every family which is being enlightened as to why it is being called upon to make such sacrifices, and the hour will come when the worst enemy of the world, of all time, will have finished his part for at least one thousand years to come. [18]

For fourteen or fifteen years I have continually proclaimed to the German nation that I regard it as my task before posterity to destroy Marxism, and that is no empty phrase but a solemn oath which I shall follow as long as I live. I have made this confession of faith, the confession of faith of a single man, that of a mighty organization. I know now that even if fate were to remove me, the fight would be fought to the end; this movement is the guarantee for that. This for us is not a fight which can be finished by compromise. We see in Marxism the enemy of our people which we will root out and destroy without mercy. . . . We must then fight to the very end those tendencies which have eaten into the soul of the German nation in the last seventeen years, which have done us such incalculable damage and which, if they had not been vanquished, would have destroyed Germany. Bismarck told us that liberalism was the pace-maker of Social Democracy. I need not say here that Social Democracy is the pace-maker of Communism. And Communism is the forerunner of death, of national destruction, and extinction. We have joined battle with it and will fight it to the death. [19]

We are enemies of cowardly pacifism because we recognize that according to the laws of nature, struggle is the father of all things. We are enemies of democracy because we recognize that an individual genius represents at all times the best in his people and that he should be the leader. Numbers can never direct the destiny of a people. Only genius can do this. We are the deadly enemies of internationalism because nature teaches us that the purity of race and the authority of the leader alone are able to lead a nation to victory. [20]

. . . Thus I am standing for exactly the same principles that I stood for already a year ago. We are convinced that a final showdown will come in this fight against Marxism. We are convinced that it must come, for two Weltanschauungen are fighting each other and there can be only one outcome! One will be destroyed and the other will win. . . . It is the great mission of the National Socialist Movement, to give this epoch a new faith and to see to it that millions will swear by this faith, so that, when some day the hour for the showdown comes, the German people will not meet the Jewish international murderers completely unarmed. [21]

Chapter Four

Nationalism

The Enlightenment saw nationalism as a positive force. It represented the integration of the masses into the political "nation". There would be an equality of nations as there was an equality of individuals. From the time of the French Revolution onwards, however, a contradiction appeared between the individualistic aspirations of nationalism and its collectivist reality.

In Germany in the nineteenth century there emerged an intelllectual nationalism based on the idea of the racial superiority of the organically unified German people (Volk). The state (Reich) represented the political expression of the union of land and people. This ideology was anti-parliamentary (representative parties disrupted the unity of the volk) and anti-capitalist (capitalism and modernity were antipathetic to the natural state of the volk). The state attained its highest state of virtue by war and the shedding of blood. To these ideologists the Jews represented all that was alien, rootless and opposed to the aristocratic and spiritual vision of nationhood. It was a scarcely altered volkish ideology which provided the basis of National Socialism. Crucially, however, the social change precipitated by the First World War nullified the aristocratic element of this volkish formula. The National Socialists coped with this ideological change in two ways. Firstly amongst the North German Strasserites the "Red" element of National Socialism was stressed, with emphasis being on the fact that the Volk was not a union of peasants ruled by aristocrats but a revolutionary union of German racial equality. Secondly the Nazis compensated for the destruction of the the old aristocracy by the creation of a new aristocracy of blood. The epitome of this new aristocracy was to be found in the organisation of the SS.

This message had its first major nineteenth century proponent in Johann Fichte who made made his Addresses to the German Nation from the

University of Berlin in 1807. Fichte told the Germans that they alone, in contrast to the decadent French and Jews, had the ability to create a new age of spiritual regeneration. 22 When it was first made this represented a message of hope to a defeated people but with the increasing power of the unified Germany as the nineteenth century progressed it came to be an ideology of success and strength. This belief system was given a scientific basis in the mid-nineteenth century by the crude adaption of social Darwinism (the intellectual development of racial Darwinism reached its apogee in 1899 with the publication of Haeckel's TheRiddle of the Universe.2 The lauding of the "volkish" German tradition was a project which could involve non-Germans who saw in the Teuton a generalised expression of the superiority of the Aryan race. One such non-German was the mystically inclined French

Nazism was a form of radical nationalism asserting absolute identity between self and nation. Hitler's ideology of Volksgemeinschaft, the community of the German people, required "overcoming bourgeois privatism" in order to "unconditionally equate the individual fate with the fate of the nation." The Volk, according to Hitler, encompassed and embraced each and every German. "No one is excepted from the crisis of the Reich," Hitler said. "There may not be a single person who excludes himself from this joint obligation." Nazism insisted that everyone was obligated to partake of the life of the community. "This Volk," Hitler declared, "is but yourselves." Nazism revolved around worship of the German nation. Hitler said: "We do not want to have any other God, only Germany." Hitler was a fanatic preacher obsessed with his god, Germany. He implored and exhorted the German people to devote their lives to the god to which he had devoted his own life: Our future is Germany. Our today is Germany. And our past is Germany. Let us take a vow this morning, at every hour, in each day, to think of Germany, of the nation, of our German people. You cannot be unfaithful to something that has given sense and meaning to your life.

Nazism represented negation of individuality in the name of the community. "You are nothing, your nation is everything," Hitler proclaimed. The moral person willingly abandoned his own desires in the name of the collective. According to Nazi ideology, one could not choose to devote one's life to one's nation or choose not to do so. Rather, renunciation of individual interests in the name of the community was a sacred obligation from which no one was exempt. The ultimate act of self-renunciation was willingness to die for Germany. Reflecting on the loyalty and devotion of his comrades, Hitler observed that "More than once, thousands and thousands of young Germans have stepped forward with self-sacrificing resolve to sacrifice their young lives freely and joyfully on the altar of the beloved fatherland." Hitler glorified the idea of "dying for one's country," building his ideology on the foundation of this commonplace idea and carrying it to an extreme, bizarre conclusion.

GERMAN NATIONALISM

Although anti-Semitism was not a powerful force in Germany compared to a number of other European nations, nationalism and militant devotion to the cultural collective was a particularly German phenomenon that paved the way for Hitler's anti-Semitic propaganda. Germany endured an identity crisis with its defeat in World War I, with its people suddenly low on patriotic energy and concerned with serious economic difficulties. It would have been unusual for any nation to express absolute faith in the greatness of their leaders after such a massive defeat, but Germany suffered more than other countries from the decrease in authoritarian sentiment among its people because this sentiment was central to the security of German pride and confidence. Authoritarianism was a necessary aspect of the German collective identity, and its relative absence during the socialist Weimar period left Germans dissatisfied and pessimistic about the future.

Nationalism had been a defining characteristic of German culture since Bismarck used his military triumphs to facilitate the birth of Germany as a unified and powerful nation. Because Germany identified itself as a land of military superiority rather than economic opportunity like the United States, the German people's focus on individual economic survival post-World War I was a threat to the overall strength of Germany as a national power. In addition to the drastic economic inflation of 1923, the Weimar Republic's structure of multiple influential political parties made the construction of a common mobilizing agenda for Germany's recovery very difficult.

The values of the German people remained as generally conservative and nationalist as they had been before the Weimar period, and the educational system taught children that Germany's signing of the Treaty of Versailles had not been a concession to defeat but rather a treacherous betrayal of the true German interest by liberalist and socialist factions. Hitler and the Nazis were an attractive solution to these frustrations with the new Weimar government because Nazi doctrine provided a convenient scapegoat for economic hardship and political disorganization: the Jews. In 1923, the same year that Germany suffered devastating inflation, Hitler was caught plotting to overthrow the Weimar government, and served only one year of his five-year prison sentence. The German people, including those in law enforcement and the legal system, were impressed with his drive and largely in agreement with his politics. Hitler had emerged with the appearance of a very sympathetic, brave, and engaging potential hero for the dissatisfied conservative middle class.

ONE RACE AND ONE NATION

Diplomat Arthur de Gobineau who between 1853–1855 wrote his Essay on the Inequality of Human Races. Gobineau's work sought the origins of Aryan superiority in bizarrely atavistic mysticism and anti-modernity. Aryan self, he believed, was hindered by Christian values, and whilst serving as ambassador to Sweden he toyed with the idea of reviving a neo-pagan cult religion. These ideas were readily received in Germany and Gobineau societies sprang up dedicated to propagating his vision of racial history.24 Other German volkish authors could not bring themselves to abandon Christianity so lightly. Paul de Lagarde (writing in Deutsche Schriften from 1873 onwards) urged the adaptation of Christianity to the Germanic character whilst effecting a programme for the destruction of urbanism, capitalism and money. Despising what he regarded as unatural political creeds he declared: "Let us not be liberal but liberated, not conservative but German." Above all, however, Lagarde detested the Jews, whom he equated with the hated powers of Capitalism. 25

This totalitarian formula was reinforced by Heinrich von Treitschke (professor of history at the University of Berlin from 1874–1896) who declared his opposition to liberal values and mercantile trade whilst singing the praises of the authoritarian power of the state and the spiritual liberation of war and violence.26 This backward looking mode of thought grew up at the time when capitalism was turning Germany into a major European power. The German intelligensia were, however, increasingly engaged in a flight from reality into the strange comforts of fantasy and myth. The German liberal poet Heinrich Heine was moved to declare:

> They conjure up the demonic powers of the ancient Germanic pantheon and because that lust to fight comes alive in them . . . a spectacle will be performed in Germany compared with which the French Revolution may look like an innocent idyll. 27

DEVOTION TO GERMANY

Das Deutsche Volk, das Deutsche Volk, das Deutsche Volk were words echoing throughout Germany in the early Thirties. Hitler's religion of Nazism permitted the German people to worship themselves, bow down to their own nation and nationality. In the United States we say, "I pledge allegiance to the flag and to the republic for which it stands, one nation, under God." The oath of the SS Man went as follows: "We swear to you, Adolf Hitler, as Fuhrer and Chancellor of the German Reich, our loyalty and bravery. We swear to you, and our superiors appointed to you, obedience unto death. So help us God!" Nazism was pledge of allegiance in its most radical form, apogee of Western nationalism.

It is misleading to conceptualize the willingness of Nazis to follow orders in terms of passive acquiescence. What we call obedience was understood and experienced by Germans as faithfulness, loyalty, and willingness to sacrifice for the community. This quality of active devotion lay at the heart of the Nazi revolution. When 15,000 persons rise to their feet and pay respect to basketball player Michael Jordan with a standing ovation, we don't call this "obedience." Rather, we understand the applause to mean that persons appreciate what Jordan has accomplished and stands for. So it was with the German people in their relation to Hitler. Many Germans loved Hitler and appreciated what he said. Hitler himself was the greatest devotee of his own religion. He declared, "We do not want to have any other God—only Germany." He inspired others to worship the god that he worshipped, indeed insisted that they do so. Though cynical and devious in his pursuit of power, his devotion to Germany was sincere and profound. Typically, he proclaimed:

> Our future is Germany. Our today is German. And our past is Germany. Let us take a vow this morning, at every hour, in each day, to think of Germany, of the nation, of our German people. You cannot be unfaithful. (19)

Hitler's nationalism insisted upon absolute identification with the community. Nazi totalitarianism meant that not a single person was exempt from the obligation to devote one's life to Germany and make enormous sacrifices in her name. Hitler said, "We are fanatic in our love for our people. We can go as loyally as a dog with those who share our sincerity, but we will pursue with fanatic hatred the man who believes that he can play tricks with this love of ours." Hitler's rage was directed toward those whom he imagined did not share his faith. The existence of such persons seemed to mock his belief and sincerity. Hitler stated that: Our aim is the dictatorship of the whole people, the community. I began to win men to the idea of an eternal national and social ideal—to subordinate one's own interests to the interest of the whole society. There are, nevertheless, a few incurables who had never understood the happiness of belonging to this great, inspiring community.

By calling persons who refused to subordinate personal interests to the interest of society "incurables," Hitler was suggesting that those who did not wish to belong to the community were suffering from a disease. This idea lay at the heart of Nazi ideology: that anyone who did not believe in Hitler and his movement, did not wish to devote his or her life to the nation, was "sick." The "disease within the body of the people" to which Hitler so often referred symbolized, we may suggest, precisely the wish to separate from the national community. It was this desire to be separate that the Nazis aspired to eradicate.

JEWISH INDIVDUALISM

If Nazism was rooted in profound attachment to Germany, Jews symbolized negation of attachment and destruction of the idea of the nation. The metaphor that appeared with greatest frequency in Hitler's speeches as a description of Jews was Zerzetzung or "force of disintegration." This German word is widely used in chemistry and biology meaning "decomposition," "decay," or "putrefaction." The word was intended to suggest that the Jewish race worked toward the destruction or decomposition of all "genuine values," of everything that was sacred to the Germans—Germanic tradition, culture, their position in the world, patriotism, and patriotic symbols. Goebbels stated in January 1945 that "The Jews are the incarnation of that destructive drive which in these terrible years rages in the enemies' warfare against everything that we consider noble, beautiful and worth preserving."

Jews symbolized for the Nazis that which called into question the fundamental beliefs and values of the German people. Where the Aryan stood for willingness to sacrifice for the community, Jews stood for individualism. If the good German was characterized by idealistic devotion to a cause, Jews represented selfishness, self-interest, practicality, and money. Goebbels contrasted "The creative, constructive philosophy of National Socialism with its idealistic goals" to the Jewish philosophy of "materialism and individualism." Jews were seen as lacking a soul—the precise opposite of the heroic, self-sacrificing Aryan.

Hitler bluntly told his audiences, "You are nothing, your nation is everything." The fundamental premise of Nazi ideology was that the individual should subordinate himself to the community. The essence of morality, according to this view, was willingness to sacrifice personal interest in the name of the nation. Hitler's Official Programme, published in 1927, put forth as its central plank: "The Common Interest before Self Interest." It stated that "The leaders of our public life all worship the same god—Individualism. Personal interest is the sole incentive." National Socialism would come into being in order to subordinate the interests of the individual to the requirements of the collective.

On the one hand, then, stood the ideal of Volksgemeinschaft, the community of the people; on the other hand stood the ideas of individualism and individuality. Hitler believed that the tendency of the individual to pursue private interest worked to shatter the bond tying him to his nation. The fundamental characteristic of Jews according to the Nazis was precisely their "free floating" quality, the fact that they lacked an organic tie to a national body. Their tendency to ruthlessly pursue personal interest (both cause and effect of their separateness) tempted others to embrace this tendency. The very existence of Jews within a nation worked to disintegrate the body politic.

The following judgment by the Cologne Labor Court dated January 21, 1941, denied the claim of Jewish employees to a vacation:

> The precondition for the claim to a vacation—membership of the plant community—does not exist. A Jew cannot be a member of the plant community on account of his whole racial tendency which is geared to forwarding his personal interests and securing economic advantages.

By virtue of the racially inherited Jewish tendency toward "forwarding personal interests and securing economic advantages," the Jew was imagined to be incapable of participating in the life of a community. Hitler called Jews the "ferment of decomposition in peoples," meaning that the Jew "destroys and must destroy." Therefore, Hitler said, it is "beside the point whether the individual Jew is 'decent' or not. In himself he carries those characteristics which Nature has given him." Hitler stated that the Jew "completely lacks the conception of an activity which builds up the life of the community." Nazi scholarship declared that the peculiar characteristic of Judaism was "its hostility to human society," which is why there could be no solution to the Jewish question. A true understanding of Jews and Judaism "insists on their total annihilation." The Jewish tendency toward selfish individualism (fixed by heredity according to the Nazis) meant that they were incapable of comprehending the necessity of national self-sacrifice. The purpose of the Final Solution was to punish the Jews for their anti-social tendencies, to demonstrate that sacrifice was required of everyone, that it was impossible for any human being to escape or resist the embrace of the nation-state. The Final Solution was undertaken in order to prove that evasion of society was impossible.

Racial Nationalism in the Twentieth Century

The work of Houston Stewart Chamberlain bridges the gap between the intellectual racism of the nineteenth century and the twentieth century reality of National Socialism. He had met and been influenced by the aging Gobineau, he became a close friend of Kaiser Wilhelm II, and on his death bed he was visited by Hitler, whom Chamberlain had earlier declared to be the "German Messiah". Chamberlain, a passionately pro-German Englishman who had married one of Wagner's daughters, was of uncertain mental stability and whilst allegedly possesed by a demon he wrote The Foundations of the Nineteenth Century which was published in 1899. This book attempted to explain German power not by reference to modern political conditions but by a retelling of ancient history using racial theory as the key. The book came to be regarded as a primary ideological text for the National Socialists. The defeat of the Germans in the First World War shattered Chamberlain's dreams of German dominance of Europe based on collective superiority. His faith, however, was restored on meeting Hitler in 1923.28 The German defeat forced many Germans to rethink their world view. For many, however, this meant a reassertion of national collectivism rather than a coming to terms with the individualism of the Weimer constitution. Oswald Spengler's Decline of the West had been written in 1911 but achieved popularity on publication in 1918 in post-war Germany. It contrasted Western civilisation (individualism, urbanism, capitalism) with German culture (collectivism, spirituality, militarism).

In order for German culture to be defended Spengler argued the nation needed to be united under an authoritarian dictator. Whilst Spengler's aristocratic Prussianism was at odds with the plebian nature of the National Socialist party much of his work provided intellectual scaffolding for the structures Hitler was to create. Similarily the writer Moeller van den Bruck, who was not anti-semitic and believed Hitler to be unsuitable to run Germany, nevertheless provided considerable ideological input to the National Socialist Movement. Bruck believed that liberalism and freedom were a symptom of cultural chaos. The role of good government was to restore authority and stability, which could only be achieved by the implementation of a new political order which Bruck christened "The Third Reich".29 As in the nineteenth century Darwinism had been harnessed to the volkish cause so in the twentieth century the new science of psychology was used to give credence to the National Socialist cause.

The Nazis found the ideas of Carl Jung, who talked of the collective or racial unconscious particularily amenable in this respect. Jung himself self talked of how he sometimes found it impossible to analyse German patients, so permeated were their minds with Judeo-Christian morality. He talked of how he dreamed that a Germanic "Wotan" figure would arise to set the Teutonic spirit free. In a similar vein Ludwig Klages wrote his psychological study The Intellect as the Antagonist of the Soul (1932) in which he stated that a heroic Germanic Siegfried was needed to set the soul of the volk free from the powers of (Jewish) rationalism.30 By the 1930's there was a solid bedrock of anti-individualist racial collectivism on which political circumstance allowed National Socialism to be built. Hitler and the other Nazi leaders did not to indulge in any act of independent creative thought in order to arm their movement with ideas. Hitler's Mein Kampf and Alfred Rosenberg's The Myth of The Twentieth Century were simply rambling reiterations of that which had been said many times before.

Chapter Five

Racism

BACK TO NATURE

While these traditions were developing in German academic and philosophical circles similar sentiments were being conveyed to a wider audience by popular literature. In German nineteenth century novels the peasant or rural artisan, spiritually rooted to the German soil, is glorified. By contrast the Jew is represented as spiritually shallow and rootless. The most famous examples of this genre are Debit and Credit by Gustav Freytag (1855) and Wilhelm Raabe's Poor Pastor (1862). The racism of these novels can be identified with the anti-capitalist volkish ideology. It can be argued that the Jew, as an alien disrupter of the volk, represented capitalism and the Jewish ghetto, which featured in many of the novels, represented the worst aspects of urbanism. The idea of an all pervading Jewish conspiracy can be seen as a symbol of the inescapable nature of capitalist progress from which the collectivist fantasies of volkish back to nature ideology were an attempt to escape.

Despite their racism, however, behind many of the nineteenth century novels was the idea that it was possible for Jews to be integrated into the German volk. In the twentieth century a hardening of racial attitudes is reflected in a body of literature which rejected any idea of Jewish assimilation and warned readers of the perils of miscegenation. Such racialism can be found in Nathanial Junger's Volk in Danger (1921) and Arthur Dinter's Sin Against Blood (1918).12 A whole genre of "Peasant" novels arose which glorified German rural life and advocated anti-Semitism. It is no accident that one of the leading "Peasant" writers of the 1920's was Dieter Eckhart who was also one of the founding members of the National Socialist party. 31 The musical work of Richard Wagner was also thoroughly permeated by volkish ideology. One of the great themes of the Ring cycle is how German heroes (the unified volk) can be corrupted by the power of gold (capitalism). Like other German artists Wagner had no qualms about equating materialism and the acquisition of wealth with the Jews. Wagner said of himself: "Perhaps I will be the last German to remain upright . . . in face of an all powerful Judaism.

In 1913 a pyramid structure was errected to commemorate the Prussian triumph over Napoleon in the "Great Battle of Peoples". Its structure was explained as representing the Nation—a concept which could not be portrayed by realism or rationality. The Germans saw the ideas of the volk confirmed to them at every level of art and philosophy. 32

AYRIANISM

The Aryan race is a concept within 19th century and 20th century European culture. It was claimed by 19th century ethnologists that 'white' European peoples originated from an ancient people called the Aryans, a name derived from the Sanskrit and Avestan word Arya, which means 'noble person'. This idea arose when linguists identified these two closely related languages as the earliest known ancestors of all the major European languages, including Latin, Greek, Germanic and Celtic. They argued that the speakers of these languages, who called themselves 'Arya' must have been the ancestors of all the European peoples. From this point the term "Aryan" came to mean something similar to "white person". It also, significantly, excluded Jewish people from 'Aryan' identity because their ancestral Hebrew language has a different origin.

The beliefs and geographical origins of the ancient Arya were much disputed at this time. Avestan was the language of ancient Persia. Sanskrit is originally associated with the Indus Valley in the north of India, just to the east of Persia. The indigenous (and modern) name for Persia, "Iran", is a variant of "Aryan" (in fact it is Ayr + -an, "land of Aryans", where -an is a suffix of location in Persian). Furthermore, the leaders of Persia called themselves Aryans. Darius the Great, King of Persia (521—486 BC), in an inscription in Naqsh-e-Rostam (near Shiraz, Iran) proclaims: ". . . I am Darius, the Great King, . . . , A Persian, son of a Persian, an Aryan, having Aryan lineage . . .". The Avesta also records a homeland, called Airyanem Vaejah (The Aryan Expanse), from which the Aryans are supposed to have migrated.

These and other findings suggested that an Aryan people whose descendants were the Achamenians (Cyrus and Darius the Great) existed and proclaimed it. However, many of these usages are also intelligible if we understand the word Aryan in its sense of 'noble'. Nevertheless many scholars accepted that the term originally identified a specific people and their culture. Certainly, an originating culture can be postulated behind those of ancient Persia and India. Other nearby peoples, notably the Hittites and Mitanni, also seem to have shared it. This culture worshipped the gods Indra, Varuna and Agni and Mithras. They also placed great emphasis on the ritualistic use of a hallucinogenic drink called Soma, extracted from an unknown plant. However, as groups separated and migrated, their religions changed. Eventually the Persian Zoroastrian and Indian Vedic faiths emerged from the primal Aryan belief-system. See also: Aryan gods.10

This evidence gave rise to the search for the original Aryan homeland, and thus, it was believed, to the origins of the European 'race'. Many scholars argued that the Aryans originated in the Inner Asian Steppes, from which they migrated both west into Europe and south into Afghanistan, Iran and parts of India around 1800 BC.

The spread of the Aryans was supposed to explain how it came to pass that Indo-European languages became so widespread throughout Europe and Asia. It was thought, moreover, that the Aryans came as conquerors, displacing earlier peoples, in most of the places where the languages were spoken. They were able to conquer so much territory because their nomadic lifestyle, their use of the horse and wheeled vehicles such as chariots gave them a decisive military advantage. This model of conquest and cultural replacement was once widely accepted, but now has generally been rejected, at least as it pertains to Europe as a whole. Conquest, if it occurred, was a local phenomenon; there is no evidence of general warfare or cultural replacements. It is also difficult to tell what language people spoke from pre-literate artifacts; where conquest has occurred, it may have been one group of Indo-Europeans by another.

Largely because of its association with Nazi and imperialist racism (see below), the term 'Aryan' is now problematic. However, in the Vedas the word is never used in a racial or ethnic sense. Arya is still used by Zoroastrians, Buddhists, and Jains, as well as Hindus, to mean "noble" or "spiritual." It is similar to the Sanskrit word sri, an epithet of respect. The claim that a distinct Aryan people once existed is still debated. In scholarly contexts the term is now only used to label the proto-culture from which the Zoroastrian and Vedic beliefs emerged. In linguistics the Indo-Aryan languages are those that derive from Sanskrit. The speakers of the original unified Indo-European language are no longer called Aryans, but are referred to as PIEs, or Proto-Indo-Europeans. However, some white supremacist groups, such as Aryan Nations, still use the term Aryan as a racial label. 5

NAZI AND IMPERIALIST USES OF THE TERM

The Russian Steppe theory of Aryan origins was not the only one circulating during the nineteenth century. Many German scholars argued that the Aryans originated in ancient Germany or Scandinavia, or at least that in those countries the original Aryan ethnicity had been preserved. It was widely believed in that the Vedic Aryans were ethnically identical to the Goths, Vandals and other ancient Germanic peoples of the Völkerwanderung. This idea was often intertwined with anti-semitic ideas. It was claimed that there were distinct 'Aryan' and 'Semitic' peoples, based on these assumptions about the linguistic and ethnic history of the ancient world. In this way Semitic peoples came to be seen as an alien presence within 'Aryan' societies. This idea evolved into the Nazi's use of the term Aryan race to refer to what they saw as being a "master race" of people of northern European descent, going so far as to murder mentally ill children in order to maintain its purity under Hitler's T-4 Euthanasia Program. This usage now has nearly no meaning outside of Nazi or neo-Nazi ideology.

In India, under the British Empire, the British rulers also used the idea of a distinct Aryan race in order to ally British power with the Indian caste system. It was argued that the Aryans were 'white' people who had invaded India in ancient times, subordinating the dark skinned native Dravidian peoples, who were pushed to the south. The Aryans had established themselves as the dominant castes. They were also the authors of the most intellectually sophisticated Vedic writings of the Hindu faith. There was thus a natural alliance between the British and the descendants of the ancient Aryans. All discussion of Aryan or Dravidian "races" remains highly controversial in India to this day, but does continue to affect political and religious debate. Some Dravidians, most commonly Tamils, claim that the worship of Shiva is a distinct Dravidian religion, to be distinguished from Brahminical "Aryan" Hinduism. In contrast, the Indian nationalist Hindutva movement denies that an Aryan invasion or migration ever occurred, arguing that Vedic beliefs emerged from the Indus Valley Civilisation, which is generally supposed to have pre-dated the advent of the Aryans in India. See also: Aryan invasion. 8

These debates also led to the Theosophical movement founded by Helena Blavatsky and Henry Olcott at the end of the nineteenth century. This was an early kind of New Age philosophy, that took inspiration from Indian culture, in particular from the Hindu reform movement the Arya Samaj founded by Swami Dayananda. The theosophs claimed the Aryans to be God's chosen race to free the world. The German Guido v. List Society later took up these ideas, mixing this ideology with nationalistic ideas. Such views also fed into the development of Nazi ideology. 10

THE LORDS OF UNREASON

The volkish irrationality on which National Socialism was based found its epitome in the occult societies which flourished in nineteenthth and early twentieth century Germany. The late nineteenth century in Germany witnessed an upsurge in occult activity. This activity took the form of a fusion of German volkish neo-pagan romanticism and the doctrine of Theosophy. The ideas of Theosophy were not native to Germany, being an Anglo-American import based on the writings of Helena Blavatsky, principally Isis Unveiled (1877) and The Secret Doctrine (1888). These works postulated a prehistoric past ruled by an elite of mystic initiates and inhabited by a succession of superior races. According to Blavatsky the latest of these superior races was the Aryans. Such ideas found a ready audience among German volkish scholars. Much of Blavatsky's work, especially in Isis Unveiled, yearns for a mystic, natural Golden Age and is a diatribe against modernity and capitalism.

A key figure in this synthesis of ideas (known as Ariosophy) was Guido Von List. List started his career as a volkish novelist. His ideas, however, became steadily more orientated towards the supernatural until he (in the tradition of Blavatsky) had created a fantastic German prehistory where the land was dominated by a secret priesthood. According to List this priesthood's secret wisdom had survived Christian persecution by means of secret societies and cryptic signs (one such sign being the swastika). In 1908 the List society was founded as a conscious attempt to establish a neo-pagan cult. When the first world war broke out List welcomed it as an opportunity for the Germans to sweep away the decadent west. Shortly after the war List died, but his ideas were carried forward by other mystic writers.9

One of List's Austrian disciples was Jorg Lanz von Liebenfels. Liebenfels mixed occult ideas with crude racial Darwinism in what was know as Theozoology. Lanz in his early career was an acknowledged expert on early Jewish religious texts and his Darwinist racial ideas were treated with some seriousness (they were published in Ernst Haekkel's Monist Journal of Racial Science). By 1908 Lanz was increasingly involved with volkish and supernatural ideas. He founded his own occult "order of the New Templars" dedicated to preserving the purity of the Aryan Race, which used the swastika as its symbol. The order's journal Ostara sold 100,000 copies in 1907. There is reliable evidence that one of its readers was Adolf Hitler. 25

Within Germany itself the many anti-semitic and volkish organisations achieved a degree of unity in 1912 when two groups were formed, the Reichammersbund and Germanenorden. Both were organised along Masonic and Listian lines and neither was very successful. The Reichhammersbund quickly foundered and under the strains of the First World War the

Germanenorden split into the "Loyalist German Order" and the "German Order Walvater".

Diplomat Arthur de Gobineau who between 1853–1855 wrote his Essay on the Inequality of Human Races. Gobineau's work sought the origins of Aryan superiority in bizarrely atavistic mysticism and anti-modernity. Aryan self, he believed, was hindered by Christian values, and whilst serving as ambasssador to Sweden he toyed with the idea of reviving a neo-pagan cult religion.) These ideas were readily received in Germany and Gobineau societies sprang up dedicated to propagating his vision of racial history. 32 German volkish authors could not bring themselves to abandon Christianity so lightly. Paul de Lagarde (writing in Deutsche Schriften from 1873 onwards) urged the adaptation of Christianity to the Germanic character whilst effecting a programme for the destruction of urbanism, capitalism and money. Despising what he regarded as unatural political creeds he declared: "Let us not be liberal but liberated, not conservative but German." Above all, however, Lagarde detested the Jews, whom he equated with the hated powers of Capitalism. 31 is totalitarian formula was reinforced by Heinrich von Treitschke (professor of history at the University of Berlin from 1874–1896) who declared his opposition to liberal values and mercantile trade whilst singing the praises of the authoritarian power of the state and the spiritual liberation of war and violence.33 This backward looking mode of thought grew up at the time when capitalism was turning Germany into a major European power. The German intelligensia were, however, increasingly engaged in a flight from reality into the strange comforts of fantasy and myth.

In Mein Kampf Hitler spoke contemptuously about "volkish wandering scholars" and on coming to power he acted to ban many occult societies. While he may have eschewed neo-paganism Hitler does, however, seem to have contemplated a personal cult in which the Bible would be replaced by Mein Kampf, the cross by the swastika and a sword would rest on the church altar. Himmler was in many ways sympathetic (to a far greater degree than Hitler) to Listian currents of thought and, under the influence of Karl Maria Wiligut, an occultist allegedly able to communicate with the Teutonic ancestors, he organised the SS along lines which would have been easily in tune with List's priesthood of the blood and Lanz's chivalrous Knights of racial purity.35

RACISM AND NAZISM

As mentioned earlier, racism (together with anti-Semitism) played a defining role in Nazi ideology. But on which ideas did this racism build? In order to answer this question it is necessary to go back to the second half of the 19th century, where many of the intellectual roots of Nazism came into existence. The Western European countries exploited their colonies in typically capitalistic fashion. This exploitation frequently resulted in the conclusion that the local population in the colonies had to be inferior individuals in order to put up with their situation. Racism, spear-headed by the writings of Charles Darwin, with time became a widely acknowledged set of thoughts that led to scientific treatises, books and research projects. Frequently this research served the purpose of pointing out the superiority or inferiority of a specific nation or race.

Based on such ideas of a racial hierarchy many European nations, including Germany, possessed a feeling that their nation was superior to everybody else. This also meant that all members of this nation should dwell within the same national borders. Such ideas can be termed 'positive racial policy'. From this come the extensive Nazi plans to move all ethnic Germans (Volksdeutsche), who were citizens of other countries, into the Third Reich.

Racist ideas were also the basis of 'negative racial policy', in the form of the exclusion of undesirable individuals from the German race. A result of this notion was the Nazi desire to remove Jews, gypsies, the handicapped, and others, from the German Volksgemeinschaft ('people's community'). This 'negative racial policy' or 'racial hygiene' was carried out systematically with great cruelty after 1933. 30

Chapter Six

Anti-Semitism

Since Jews were over-represented in the professions of banking and medicine in Germany, conservative non-Jews already had reason to resent their success and to worry that Jews were secretly plotting to take over the nation. Old myths of a Jewish conspiracy and Jews sacrificing Christian children in ritual ceremonies were recycled. These rumors were similar to the rhetoric of Christian fundamentalists in the United States, beginning in the Reagan era, about the widespread secret torture and murder of children by Satanic cults. The 1935 Nazi policy of requiring citizens to carry ID cards to indicate their Aryan status generated a tendency toward self-ghettoization in the Jews in order to avoid being publicly persecuted for not having ID cards, as well as more anti-Semitism among non-Jewish Germans. Aryan ID cards were an effective psychological technique to make the people subscribe to an "us-them" view and to see Jews as criminals. Legal methods were not the only strategies employed by the Nazi government to heighten anti-Semitism in Germany. Just as the fear of Satanists was encouraged in the United States by the non-secular pseudo-scientific phenomenon of "recovered memory therapy" in which adults were lead to recall being victimized by cults, Nazi arguments of anti-Semitism were legitimized by the scientific community's enthusiasm for the study of eugenics. 18

Both recovered memory therapy and eugenics were products of cultural bias and scapegoating; they were convincing as scientific advances and accepted by distinguished academic personalities. Eugenics, incidentally, began in the United States and was adopted by German thinkers as a strategy for empirical validation of cultural elitism. Because of Hitler's influence, social Darwinism in Germany took on a strong anti-Semitic aspect that was not as

prominent in the United States, where malignant social interpretations of evo-
lutionary theory were used primarily against blacks.

Prior to the Nazis' focus on Jews as a genetically inferior race, anti-Semitism
in Germany and the rest of Europe was based in a religious context. Theologians
and philosophers from St. Augustine and Origean to Martin Luther asserted that
the Jews had killed God and that the Jewish religion was primitive and amoral.
Forced conversion to Protestantism was the primary method used to persecute
Jews before the twentieth century and the influence of eugenics. The basic anti-
Semitism behind religious and racial persecution was the same, Friedlander
says, but the additional ingredient of modern science in Nazi ideology con-
tributed to the more potent and destructive manifestation of their hatred of Jews
compared to earlier incidents of religious discrimination. 26 The reason for the
increased dangerous potential of race-based anti-Semitism was the uselessness
of religious conversion as a solution to the "Jewish problem" once Jews were
presented as a biological threat to the well-being of "true Germans." By the
Third Reich, science had replaced religion as the top authority on knowledge and
truth, and Jews were seen as a contaminated race of people whose genetic flaws
could not be remedied with religious doctrine. In this case, the Enlightenment
had not only failed to fight ignorance, but meticulously dressed it up in the em-
peror's new clothing of empiricism.

Hitler, of course, was a major player in re-focusing anti-Semitism onto the
issue of race, since his hatred of the Jews had little to do with their religious
beliefs. Hitler himself was an atheist. He ultimately planned to eradicate all
religion, including Protestant Christianity, from German society. This goal is
understandable in light of Hitler's utter lack of compassion and moral con-
science, both of which are important tenets of Christianity. The Protestant majority nonetheless trusted Hitler to be sympathetic to their ethics. Unlike the
Catholic minority, German Protestants were believers in modernism and
Cartesian rationalism, which meant they were excited about scientific
progress in the area of eugenics. They were wary of liberalism and often concerned about hidden Communist influence in the Weimar government. They
liked Hitler's promises of a thriving economy and the exclusion of welfare
dependents and criminals from German society. They were not, however, in
favor of mass murder as a eugenic strategy. This was an extremist and violent
notion that would have been horrifying to the average middle class German
citizen. Had Hitler not been clever enough after 1928 to avoid mentioning in
his public speeches any explicitly anti-Semitic doctrine, the people of Germany might not have believed his false projected image as the nation's benev-
olent savior.

When Hitler was appointed Chancellor in 1933, the people's enthusiastic
approval was for his energetic devotion to bringing back the German spirit of

military efficiency, faith in authority, and political conservatism. Hitler's true self, the megalomaniac and mass murderer, was not visible to most people at that time, but those who did know this aspect of Hitler counted on it to make their fanatical desire for the annihilation of Jews a reality. These fellow Nazis, particularly Dietrich Eckhardt and the other original members of the reactionary German Workers Party, had deliberately cultivated Hitler's private sadism as well as his public persona, and envisioned him as an ideal human bridge between their extreme agenda and the German people's need for economic and social revitalization of their beloved nation .36 Hitler was socially skilled, a natural orator, and a laid-back politician whose speeches generated energy and optimism rather than alienating audiences with sinister plans as Eckhardt likely would have. He was also a veteran and came from a working-class background, qualities that made it possible for the people to relate to him as one of their own kind and to trust him not to abuse his authority. Hitler's strong authoritarian presence did not put people off, because they felt their country needed an executive force to rebuild the culture of organization and obedience that was the essence of Germany. At first, Hitler and the Nazi party seemed likely to change economic and social conditions for the better, and therefore it was difficult for the German majority not to minimize to themselves the fact that their gain was coming at a great cost to persecuted minority groups. Denial was also aided by the seclusion of Jews in ghettos where their suffering could not be seen, and then by deportation of the Jews to other nations when the Final Solution went into action in 1941. At that time, the mass killings of Jews were easily legitimized within the unique context of World War II. 37

Christopher Browning argues that "nothing helped the Nazis to wage a race war so much as the war itself. . . Ordinary Germans did not have to be 'of one mind' with Hitler's demonological view of the Jews to carry out genocide (216)." Killing enemies during a war is normal behavior, and Hitler was able to convince the German people that Jews were their enemy. The Regime also found that when they defeated other nations in the war, the Jews of those nations became Germany's responsibility, and their numbers were too great for them all to be deported and ghettoized in Poland or Madagascar. Germany already had its own large population of impoverished Jews with nowhere to live as a result of The Goering/Himmler solution of 1938 to take away all their property. It was becoming impossible to solve the "Jewish problem" via mass deportation; the next step was interment in concentration camps. Auschwitz became the first death camp in 1941. 33

In addition, the military operations of the Final Solution did not require individuals outside the Nazi party to play a large part in its implementation; rather, they were each only responsible for small pieces of the overall task that, in themselves, did not produce guilt or horror in the workers who carried out these specific duties. It was natural for German soldiers not to be inclined to look at the bigger picture of what they were doing, because they were trained, both directly by the military and indirectly by their culture, to carry out orders without questioning the authority figures who gave them. Hitler's clever propaganda, delivered to the people since the beginning of his dictatorship, encouraged Germans to remain locked in this highly militaristic and loyal state of mind. 26

ANTI-SEMITISM AND NAZISM

The Nazis did not invent Anti-Semitism nor did they conceive or concoct many of the images and caricatures that Jews were subjected to in the 12 Nazi years of terror and tyranny. For centuries Christian countries persecuted Jews.

- Pogroms (legalised and police promoted riots) raged in the Russia
- In France, the Jews had suffered indignity after the trial of Alfred Dreyfus, a Jewish General wrongly accused and sentenced for falsely selling French army secrets. The crowds at his trial did not shout, 'death to Dreyfus' but ". . . Death to the Jews. . .".
- In Germany, the Jew was granted equal legal status under the constitution of the Weimar Republic (1919). This did not always translate to actual status and equality but nonetheless it was a change that Jews in Germany had not expected.

When Hitler arrived in power (1933) he had made no secret in the pervious years of his distaste and hatred of the Jew. He made no secret of his desire for the removal of their rights and properties and expulsion from Germany entirely. At the core of Hitler's ideology lay his conception of the German nation as a gigantic organism or actual body politic. This precious organism was imagined to be under attack, its life threatened by the presence of the Jew whose continued presence within the nation would lead to the death of Germany. Hitler described the Jew typically as the "demon of the disintegration of peoples, symbol of the unceasing destruction of their lives." In order to rescue Germany and save the life of the body politic, it was necessary to eliminate from within the nation those forces that threatened to destroy it. Genocide grew out of Hitler's conviction that in order to save the life of Germany it was necessary to exterminate the Jewish people. 32

Hitler believed that his project was of the utmost value, indeed the most significant mission that a human being could undertake. He stated that he wished to "prevent our Germany from suffering, as Another did, the death upon the Cross." In order to achieve his objective—to save Germany from death—everything was permissible:

> We may be inhumane, but if we rescue Germany we have achieved the greatest deed in the world. We may work injustice, but if we rescue Germany then we have removed the greatest injustice in the world. We may be immoral, but if our people is rescued we have once more opened the way for morality.

To rescue Germany would be to achieve "the greatest deed in the world." Hitler's struggle (Kampf) was the struggle against death: to maintain the life of Germany in the face of forces that he believed were acting to destroy her. Hitler often stated that the purpose of National Socialism was to "maintain the life of Germany." He conceived of this mission in biological terms. Germany was described as a living organism with the German people constituting the cells of this organism. Jews constituted cells (bacteria or viruses) whose continued presence within the national body would lead to disease and death. In Mein Kampf, Hitler stated that Germans would choose as their leader one who "profoundly recognizes the distress of his people" and who, after he has attained "the ultimate clarity" with regard to the nature of the disease, "seriously tries to cure it." Hitler believed he was that unique politician who possessed the insight to diagnose Germany's disease and the determination to prescribe and carry out the necessary treatment. 9

Hitler posed the question, "Could anyone believe that Germany alone was not subject to exactly the same laws as all other human organisms?" In his diary on March 27, 1942, Goebbels described the process of extermination as "pretty barbaric and not to be described in detail" but denied that it was necessary to have compunctions because after all this was a "life-and-death struggle between the Aryan race and the Jewish bacillus." In his 1935–6 propaganda booklet Himmler observed that the battle against peoples conducted by Jews had belonged "so far as we can look back, to the natural course of life on our planet." Therefore one could "calmly reach the conviction" that the struggle of nations against Jews, of "life and death" was quite as much a law of nature as "man's struggle against some epidemic, as the struggle of a healthy body to eliminate plague bacillus." 33 What was the meaning of this biological imagery employed by Nazi leaders? What did Hitler have in mind when he stated that Germany was subject to the same laws as "all other human organisms?" What was the "law of nature," as Himmler put it that made the struggle of nations against Jews equivalent to the struggle of a healthy body against the "plague bacillus?" The law to which Hitler and Himmler were referring, I believe, was the law of the immune system, that mechanism operating biochemically within each organism that works to destroy each and every cell identified as "not self." 34

Jews in the mind of Hitler and other Nazi leaders represented a foreign microorganism within the bloodstream of Germany.

Since Jews were virulent microorganisms within the body politic, it was necessary that every single one of them be destroyed, lest they begin again to divide and multiply. The SS men functioned as "killer cells" within the national organism, assigned the task of identifying, tracking down and destroying the dangerous microorganisms. On the evening of February 22, 1942, Hitler met with Himmler and a Danish SS major and expounded his conviction that;

> The discovery of the Jewish virus is one of the greatest revolutions that has taken place in the world. The battle in which we are engaged today is of the same sort as the battle waged, during the last century, by Pasteur and Koch. How many diseases have their origin in the Jewish virus! We shall regain our health only by eliminating the Jew. Hitler conceived of the Final Solution from the perspective of immunology. As "Doctor of the German people,"

He would act to save the life of the body politic by destroying the pathogens that were the source of Germany's disease. 38

Nazism, then, revolved around the idea that Germany was an actual body whose life was endangered by the presence of foreign cells within its bloodstream. The Final Solution represented a systematic effort to remove these alien cells from within the body politic, thereby destroying the source of the nation's disease and saving its life. This was the central fantasy contained within Hitler's ideology: That Germany was an actual organism containing Jewish bacteria and viruses whose removal was necessary if the nation was to survive. However, what is the meaning of this extraordinary idea? Nations are not bodies and Jews are not bacteria. Why did these metaphors resonate with the German people? Let us approach this question by viewing Nazism as a religion. 39

THE HOLOCAUST

The extermination of the Jewish people began in 1941, prior to the development of death camps and gas chambers. As the German army penetrated into the Soviet Union, they were followed closely by the Einsatzgruppen or mobile killing units. It is estimated that more than one-and-one-half million Jews were killed, most of them shot at close range. By the end of the winter of 1941–42, more than 90% of the Jews trapped by the Germans east of the Soviet border had been killed. The extermination of men, women, and children apparently did not disturb Hitler. "If I don't mind sending the pick of the German people into the hell of war without regret for the shedding of valuable German blood," he said, "Then I have naturally the right to destroy millions of men of inferior races who increase like vermin." 40 The logic of extermination seems to be contained within this statement. If he had the right as commander-in-chief of the army to send the best human beings, German soldiers, to their deaths, why, Hitler reflected, would he not have the right to send Jews, the worst human beings, mortal enemies of the German people to their deaths?

A sign at the entrance to Auschwitz read: "I bid you welcome. This is not a holiday resort but a labor camp. Just as our soldiers risk their lives at the front to gain victory for the Third Reich, you will have to work here for the welfare of a new Europe." This sign, mocking or taunting the Jews as they arrived at the camps, evokes the mentality that generated the Holocaust. It would appear that the Final Solution functioned as a means of conveying to Jews the following message: "41 Do not think that you are exempt from the obligation to sacrifice for Germany. Just as our soldiers are suffering and dying for Germany at the front, so you too will be compelled to suffer and die in the camps." Jews—like the German soldiers—would be required to give over their bodies and to sacrifice their lives at the behest of the nation-state.

The Final Solution came into being in order to teach Jews a lesson, punish them for their "selfish individualism." Jews symbolized the idea that it was possible to evade or escape the nation-state, to function or exist under conditions of separateness from the community. The Final Solution represented an effort to demonstrate that there could be no such thing as separation from the national community. The Holocaust affirmed that the nation-state was "total," capable of controlling the lives and deaths of each and every human being within its boundaries. The Final Solution came into being in order to substantiate the omnipotence of Germany, show the Jews "once and for all" that they were not exempt from the obligation to submit to the community. 42 The logic of the Holocaust followed from the logic of domination and death that was the essence of National Socialism. Nazism glorified the nation-state and negated the individual, conferring absolute power upon the idea of the "community." In Nazism, the human being was expected to sacrifice his concrete existence for the good of the nation. Hitler explained to the German people their role, and summed up Nazi ideology as follows: "You are nothing, your nation is everything." On the other hand according to Hitler there was one group of people, Jews, that was incapable of catching on, who refused to buy into the ideal of sacrificial submission. The idea that certain persons believed that they were exempt from the obligation to submit to the community—enraged Hitler and was the source of what followed.43 Why were some people required to give over their lives, to sacrifice themselves for Germany while others were not? Hitler projected the idea of freedom from the community onto the Jews.

However, the Nazis could not bear to contemplate freedom, the idea that some people were not required to surrender their lives to the state. After all, they had sworn "obedience unto death" to Hitler and Germany. The Final Solution was undertaken in order to demonstrate that freedom was not an option, that it was impossible to evade the nation-state. The Holocaust came into being in order to demonstrate to the Jews that Germany was omnipotent. No one was capable of resisting; everyone would be compelled to submit. If German soldiers were suffering and dying in massive numbers in battle, so Jews would be required to suffer and die in massive numbers in death camps. The Holocaust represented the consummation of Nazism, the climax of Western nationalism, and fulfillment of the fantasy that it is "good and beautiful to die for one's country." By acting out this fantasy of nationalism, taking it to its extreme, bizarre conclusion, Hitler was telling us something about, pointing toward the rottenness or corruptness of this fantasy. In war, soldiers are required to give over their bodies and souls to the nation-state, to die when leaders ask them to do so. The Holocaust constituted an extension of this logic. Jews were compelled to give over their bodies and souls to Germany. The Holocaust depicts the idea of "dying for the country" stripped of words such as honor, loyalty and glorify. 44

THE JEWISH QUESTION

Upon returning home after having been discharged from a military hospital as cured, Hitler alleged that the "offices were filled with Jews." He claimed that "nearly every clerk was a Jew and nearly every Jew was a clerk." Hitler was amazed at this "plethora of warriors of the chosen people and could not help compare them with their rare representatives at the front." Thus the question of why some had died in the war and others had not, why the best had been killed while the worst survived, mutated into: "Why while German soldiers were dying at the front were Jews safe, comfortable and secure at home?" Hitler believed that during the time German soldiers were fighting the war, Jews at home who avoided joining the army had fomented revolution and taken over the government. Hitler became filled with fantasies of revenge. He put forth an enigmatic idea linking the death of German soldiers at the front with the murder of Jews. In Mein Kampf, Hitler said, "If the best men were dying at the front, the least we could do was to wipe out the vermin."45

He declared that "if at the beginning of the War and during the War twelve or fifteen thousand of these Hebrew corrupters of the people had been held under poison gas, as happened to hundred of thousands of our very best German workers in the field, the sacrifice of millions at the front would not have been in vain." It would appear that Hitler attempted to come to terms with the meaning of the First World War by suggesting that the death of millions of Germans soldiers would become bearable if only Jews too were compelled to die. Hitler's vision of war and genocide constituted an ideology of death insisting that no one should be exempt from the obligation to sacrifice one's life for the national community. Further, it would appear that the Holocaust grew directly out of Hitler's experience of the First World War. Hitler and his comrades had been subjected to poison gas in the trenches during the First World War. In the spirit of do unto others as has been done unto you, Hitler would subject Jews to poison gas in the death camps. 4

The Holocaust expressed Hitler's idea that no one should be allowed to escape or evade the obligation to sacrifice one's life for Germany. Hitler believed that the best human beings had been killed in the First World. War while the worst had survived. In the Second World War the worst human beings would not be spared. Just as German soldiers were required to give over their bodies and lives to the nation-state, so Jews would be required to do so. Anti-Semitism can be translated with 'hostility towards Jews'. The Nazis' hatred for the Jews and the use of the Jew as a universal explanation for all Germany's problems is unique. Fascism—i.e. Nazism's Italian counterpart— does not include this element. 47 The Nazi ideology went one step further, however, in its idea of the Jews' worldwide conspiracy to cause the downfall of the Aryan race: Via ingenious explanations, the Jews were matched with the Soviet Bolshevists, thus creating 'Judeo-Bolshevism'. It was the Nazi Party's chief ideologist, Alfred Rosenberg, who was able to invent this combination and thus really making the Jews 'the world's biggest crook'. Now all of a sudden, American-Jewish lobbyists and the Bolshevist enemy in the Soviet Union were two sides of the same coin! The notion is of course absurd, but it was nevertheless extremely useful as a propaganda tool during the war, in particular following the United States' entry. One of the most prominent points of Hitler's ideology was his belief in the "pure Aryan race," which was superior to all other world races. This belief led to one of the most featured aspects of the Nazi rule. The word "Aryan," which literally denoted any group of Indo-European speakers of the Aryan language, was to become a convenient tool for Hitler's ideals of pan-Germanism. 48 He proclaimed that all people of true German, or "Aryan," descent were true German citizens. By the same law, all people residing in the German state who were not of pure German lineage would not be considered citizens. The Nazis, under Hitler, set out to "Aryanize" Germany by removing other races from control of big business in the country. Eventually, the attempts to Aryanize extended as far as the act of removing Polish children of Aryan appearance from their families for adoption by German families. 49

This program began quite legally. Hitler and the Nazis formed and passed laws, with the power of the Enabling Act, which at first encumbered and finally destroyed Jewish businesses in Germany and Austria. Laws were passed which forbade Jews from working in government jobs, followed by laws boycotting Jewish businesses altogether. Finally, in 1935, the Nazis held a conference at Nuremburg which ended with a law denying citizenship to any "racial" Jews, even if they were to convert to Christianity. 50 Even families that had long ago converted were judged on lineage alone. Hitler was eventually to develop an entire office within his government that was dedicated to tracing lineage, and if a person was found to have had even one person within his family that was Jewish by blood, his rights of citizenship were stripped from him.

Krystallnacht, or "the Night of Shattered Glass," an internally organized pogrom against Jewish businesses, was perhaps the first major insight into Hitler's determination to completely rid the country of Jews. This undertaking, organized by Hitler's S.A., was a decisive move in the Aryanization and "purification" of Germany and Austria which would become law in Nazi Germany. Hitler's ideals of an Arayn nation and pure German race, enforced by violence, were being realized. 51 The fact that they were all pursued in a legal context discouraged most resistance that may have arisen against the Nazis.

ANTI-SEMITISM IN THEORY

Anti-Semitism became the dominant element conceiving of Germanness as threatened by gradual disintegration through the Jewish race. Hitler called for the defense of "Blood and Soil" (Blut und Boden), the annihilation of the Jews and the strengthening of the Nordic race which was to rule over its "inferiors" as the "Master race". National Socialism emphasized the element of das Volk (the people as nation race), demanded unconditional surrender of the individual to the "community" (you are nothing, your people is everything), and preached a charismatic "faith in the leader" ("Führer, give the command, we shall follow"). It adopted impulse proceeding from the pre-First World War youth movement (romanticism of communal experience), glorified the comradeship of combat in war, and took on Communist and Fascist characteristics. The "movement" became a vortex for the discontented, who were disillusioned by parliamentary democracy and supported the demands of the NSDAP for autarchy in economic life, and expansionist foreign policy (Volk ohne Raum = a people without living space), liberation from the "bondage of the Versailles dictate", and the combating of Bolshevik tendencies. 52

ALFRED ROSENBERG'S
MYTH OF THE TWENTIETH CENTURY (1935)

Finally, the racial doctrine upon which this ideology rested in large part can be seen through the eyes of the party's "ideologist"—Alfred Rosenberg: Alfred Rosenberg discussed the relationship between the state and the "Volk" in his Myth of the Twentieth Century (1935):

> The state is nowadays no longer an independent idol, before which everything must bow down; the state is not even an end but is only a means for the preservation of the "Volk" . . . Forms of the state change, and the laws of the state pass away; the folk remains. From this alone follows that the nation is the first and last, that to which everything else has to be subordinated.
>
> The new thought puts folk and race higher than the state and its forms. It declares protection of the folk more important than protection of a religious denomination, a class, the monarchy, or the republic; it sees in treason against the folk a greater crime than high treason against the state. No "Volk" of Europe is racially unified, including Germany. In accordance with the newest researches, we recognize five races, which exhibit noticeably different types. Now it is beyond question true that the Nordic race primarily has borne the genuine cultural fruits of Europe. The great heroes, artists, founders of states have come from this race. . . . Nordic blood created German life above all others. Even those sections, in which only a small part today is pure Nordic, have their basic stock from the Nordic race. Nordic is German and has functioned so as to shape the culture and human types of the westisch, dinarisch, and ostisch-Baltisch races. Also a type which is predominantly dinarisch has often been innerly formed in a Nordic mode. This emphasis on the Nordic race does not mean a sowing of "race-hatred" in Germany, but on the contrary, the conscious acknowledgment of a kind of racial cement within our nationality. 53
>
> . . . On the day when Nordic blood should completely dry up, Germany would fall to ruin, would decline into a characterless chaos. That many forces are consciously working toward this, has been discussed in detail.
>
> For this they rely primarily on the Alpine lower stratum, which, without any value of its own, has remained essentially superstitious and slavish despite all Germanization. Now that the external bond of the old idea of the Reich has fallen away, this blood is active, together with other bastard phenomena, in order to put itself in the service of a magic faith or in the service of the democratic chaos, which finds its herald in the parasitic but energetic Judaism.

The foundation for the arising of a new aristocracy lies in those men who have stood—in a spiritual, political, and military sense—in the foremost positions in the struggle for the coming Reich. It will appear thereby with inner necessity that up to 80 per cent of these men will also externally approach the Nordic type, since the fulfillment of the demanded values lies on a line with the highest values of this blood. With the others the inheritance, which exhibits itself in actions, outweighs personal appearance. 54

Europe's states have all been founded and preserved by the Nordic man. This Nordic man through alcohol, the World War, and Marxism has partially degenerated, partially been uprooted. . . . In order to preserve Europe, the Nordic energies of Europe must first be revitalized, strengthened. That means then Germany, Scandinavia with Finland, and England.

. . . Nordic Europe is the fated future, with a German central Europe. Germany as racial and national state, as central power of the continent, safe-guarding the south and southeast; the Scandinavian states with Finland as a second group, safe-guarding the northeast; and Great Britain, safe-guarding the west and overseas at those places where required in the interest of the Nordic Man. [7]

RUSSIAN JEWISH REVOLUTION

"Does it not occur to you that the Jews, even without your help, are citizens of a state mightier and more powerful than any of yours, and that if you give them in addition citizenship in your states, they will trample your other citizens under foot?" Fichte addressed the German nation a hundred years ago with this insight. (15).

The Protocols of the Elders of Zion was an infamous forgery apparently based upon a series of notes for the sessions of the World Zionist congress in Basle in 1897. The participants appeared to be plotting the overthrow of national governments, the establishment of a Jewish world state of an authoritarian nature, and the imposition of Judaism on a world scale. The origins of this book go as far back into the nineteenth century, but the version that became familiar in Germany was concocted in Russia around 1905 and was brought to Germany by members of the Tsarist secret police fleeing the Bolshevik revolution. In Germany the Protocols was an immediate success, the first edition sold more than 120,000 copies. At the same time

Theodor Fritsch, a leading anti-Semitic publisher and editor of Der Hammer, brought out apopular version in Leipzig. Although, it was proved to be a forgery by the New York Times in 1921, the Protocols gained worldwide fame and became particularly popular in Germany, where the idea of a Jewish world conspiracy made a powerful appeal, both to frustrated nationalism and, more specifically, to the various German anti-Semitic movements.

Rosenberg, Hitler's deputy while he was in prison, wrote the "The Folkish Idea of State" contains an effort at a racial theory of culture, history and politics. The goal is a classless, racially integrated, culturally creative society is set forth; when this is achieved, a thoroughly expansionist foreign policy can follow. 15

The Frenchman Gobineau and the Englishman Chamberlain were inspired by our concept of a new order-a new order, I tell you, or if you prefer, an ideological glimpse into history in accordance with the basic principle of the blood. We do not judge by merely artistic or military standards or even by purely scientific ones. We judge by the spiritual energy which a people is capable of putting forth, which will enable it in ten years to recapture what it has lost in a thousand years of warfare. I intend to set up a thousand year Reich and anyone who supports me in battle is a fellow-fighter for a unique spiritual-I would almost say divine-creation. At the decisive moment the decisive factor is not the ratio of strength but the spiritual force employed. Betrayal of the nation is possible even when no crime has been committed, in other words when a historical mission has not been fulfilled. 56

This statement by Hitler gives rise to several intriguing questions. What was the "basic principle of the blood" which inspired Hitler's "new order"? What did he mean by the "spiritual energy" of the people and how was it connected to their blood? Why did Hitler envision his movement as generating a "spiritual" and even "divine creation" that would fulfill a "historic mission"? What was the relationship between "the basic principle of the blood" and Hitler's fanatical hatred of Jews? And finally, what were the sources of these ideas, assuming of course that Hitler was influenced by the philosophies of others? Is it possible that occult or esoteric racial philosophy may, in fact, have been one of the major sources for Hitler's racial ideology?

It is evident from Mein Kampf and Hitler's speeches that he viewed racial conflict as the determining factor in all of human history. "The racial question gives the key not only to world history, but to all human culture." 57 Race was not simply a political issue to be used to curry the favor of the masses, but the "granite foundation" 58 of Hitler's ideology. Hitler's racial ideology stemmed from what he called "the basic principle of the blood." This meant that the blood of every person and every race contained the soul of a person and likewise the soul of his race, the Volk. Hitler believed that the Aryan race, to which all "true" Germans belonged, was the race whose blood (soul) was of the highest degree. God Himself had, in fact, created the Aryans as the most perfect men, both physically and spiritually. 59

Since the blood (soul) of the Aryans contained specific spiritual energies, the "cultural energies" or "racial primal elements," 60 as Hitler often called them, the Aryans supplied the culture that creates the beauty and dignity of

higher humanity. In other words, all that man calls higher culture was ultimately the product of the spiritual and creative energies that exist in the blood
of the Aryans. Hitler stated:

> All the human culture, all the results of art, science, and technology that we see
> before us today, are almost exclusively the creative product of the Aryan. This
> very fact admits of the not unfounded inference that he alone was the founder of
> all higher humanity, therefore representing the prototype of all that we under-
> stand by the word "man." He is the Prometheus of mankind from whose bright
> forehead the divine spark of genius has sprung at all times. . . . Exclude him—
> and perhaps after a few thousand years darkness will again descend on the earth,
> human culture will pass, and the world turn to a desert.61 Human culture and
> civilization on this continent are inseparably bound up with the presence of the
> Aryan. If he dies out or declines, the dark veils of an age without culture will
> again descend on this globe. 62

Indeed, this dying-off of the Aryans was what Adolf Hitler perceived as
happening around him. Germany's loss of World War I and subsequent economic problems were the visible contemporary evidence of Aryan decline.
This descent occurred by the original sin of blood poisoning, or the contamination of the Aryan blood (soul) by an inferior race: The Aryan gave up the
purity of his blood and, therefore, lost his sojourn in the paradise which he
had made for himself. He became submerged in the racial mixture, and gradually, more and more, lost his cultural capacity, until at last, not only mentally
but also physically, he began to resemble the subjected aborigines more than
his own ancestors. . . . Thus cultures and empires collapsed to make place for
new formations. Blood mixture and the resultant drop in the racial level is the
sole cause of the dying out of old cultures; for men do not perish as a result
of lost wars, but by the loss of that force of resistance which is contained only
in pure blood. All who are not of good race in this world are chaff. 63

The "serpent" that brought about the contamination of pure Aryan blood
was, of course, the Jew. "The mightiest counterpart to the Aryan is represented by the Jew."9 To Hitler, the Jews were, of course, not members of a
particular religious creed, but a specific race: The Jew has always been a people with definite racial characteristics and never a religion; only in order to
get ahead he early sought for a means which could distract unpleasant atten-
tion from his person. And what would have been more expedient and at the
same time more innocent than the "embezzled" concept of a religious community? For here, too, everything is borrowed or rather stolen. Due to his own
original special nature, the Jew cannot possess a religious institution, if for no
other reason because he lacks idealism in any form, and hence belief in a
here-after is absolutely foreign to him. And a religion in the Aryan sense can-

not be imagined which lacks the conviction of survival after death in some form. 64

From Hitler's perspective the Jewish race was not created by God as one of the original root races of mankind and was, in his mind, un-Godly, inhuman, the embodiment of all that was evil. Hence the Jew " . . . stops at nothing, and in his vileness he becomes so gigantic that no one need be surprised if among our people the personification of the devil as the symbol for all evil assumes the living shape of the Jew." 65 The goal of the Jews was the domination of the world, a task that could be achieved by the poisoning of Aryan blood. Hitler contended that the Jews used a variety of methods to accomplish this task. The most blatant was miscegenation, accomplished by Jewish "rape" of Aryan girls and Jewish importation of Blacks into Germany in order to further destroy Aryan purity and carry out this kind of "disarming" of the spiritually leading class "of his racial adversaries." 66

To Hitler, the Jewish race was also attempting to poison the Aryan blood (soul) by utilizing social methods, such as cultural and political means. The Jew was the fundamental cause of the decadence that Hitler saw in modern art and literature. To Hitler, Jewish modem art was a deliberate attempt to infect the unconsciousness or inner self of the Aryan people. "Culturally he contaminates art, literature, the theater, makes a mockery of natural feeling, overthrows all concepts of beauty and sublimity, of the noble and the good, and instead drags men down into the sphere of his own base nature." 67 But it is in the area of politics that Hitler perceived the greatest Jewish threat to the Aryan race. Jewish infiltration of the bourgeoisie had made the latter puppets for the execution of the Jewish plan for world domination. Thus the bourgeois economic institution of capitalism and the political institutions of liberalism, democracy, parliamentarianism, freedom of the press, and internationalism were all Jewish instruments creating disorder in the world as a stepping stone to domination. 68 By far the most powerful political tool of the Jewish race, however, was Marxism. Marxism was a rival Weltanschauung that created a "view of life" directly hostile to everything in which Hitler believed. Marxism, to Hitler, maintained that the state had in itself the "creative, culture-forming force," 69 meaning that the state created a nation's culture out of economic necessities. In Hitler's view, the state could not create a nation's culture. Since the nation was the outward manifestation of a race's (Volk's) inner nature of soul, the state then could only be the instrument by which a race could express its cultural energies. The state's primary function was to preserve and promote those Aryan culture-creating spiritual elements that existed in the blood of the Aryan race.

The state is a means to an end. Its end lies in the preservation and advancement of a community of physically and psychically homogeneous creatures. This preservation itself comprises first of all existence as a race and thereby permits the free development of all the forces dormant in this race. . . . Thus, the highest purpose of a folkish state is concern for the preservation of those original racial elements which bestow culture and create the beauty and dignity of a higher mankind. We, as Aryans, can conceive of the state only as the living organism of a nationality which not only assures the preservation of this nationality, but by the development of its spiritual and ideal abilities leads it to the highest freedom. 70 Hitler also deplored Marxism for its belief in racial equality. Obviously racial inequality and Aryan domination did not permit such misunderstanding of the role of race in history. Likewise, Hitler denounced Marxism's levelling egalitarianism, which he felt destroyed the natural principle of inequality and the consequent domination of some individuals (an elite) over others .71

Hitler saw the Marxist threat to Aryan culture-creating ability not as coincidental but as a deliberate plan to destroy culture, bring civilization into chaos, and enable the Jews to achieve their goal of world domination. To Hitler, "the Jew Karl Marx" knew precisely what policies would lead to world chaos. Actually Karl Marx was only the one among millions who, with the sure eye of the prophet, recognized in

the morass of a slowly decomposing world the most essential poisons, extracted them, and, like a wizard, prepared them into a concentrated solution for the swifter annihilation of the independent existence of free nations on this earth. And all this in service of his race. 72

In conjunction with his racial ideology and antisemitism, Hitler often spoke of an "historic" or "higher mission" of the Aryan race and its elite core, the German people. The Aryans, according to Hitler, were once rulers of the earth, the highest race of mankind, endowed with the highest degree of spiritual qualities and the only ones capable of producing a higher civilization. 73 Aryans were, in essence, god-men on earth, but through blood poisoning lost their ruling position. However, as its "higher mission," the German people were destined to regain this position for the Aryan race. To do so, Germany must restructure its political and social foundations and create a state whose function was to promote the Aryan culturecreating "spiritual elements" that exist in the blood of the German race. If this were done, racially and thus spiritually pure human beings could be produced, ensuring Aryan world domination. 74

But if this Aryan destiny were to be fulfilled, Hitler believed, one major obstacle would have to be dealt with-the Jew. The Jew was the poisoner of the blood (soul) of the Aryan race, thus inhibiting its spiritual growth and endangering its divine destiny. Since Hitler saw all Jewish actions as racially and thus spiritually motivated, it became his divine mission to create an Aryan spiritual movement to combat the Jewish race 75 Hitler believed that his Nazi party, founded as a spiritual movement, would successfully rise to German political dominance since it was based in his mind on eternally true ideals rooted in the very soul of the Aryan race.76 Once in power, the Nazi movement could then create a state that would foster the historic destiny of the Aryan race. And the first task of this Aryan state would be to eliminate the Jewish threat. 77 This is why Hitler's political career both began and ended with a warning against the Jewish danger. In a letter dated 16 September 1919, called "the first piece of writing of Hitler's political career," Hitler was quite clear about his motives: the "ultimate goal [of a rational antisemitism] must unalterably be the elimination of the Jews altogether."

At the very end of his career, when he wrote his political testament to the German people, his preoccupation with the Jewish threat was still uppermost in his mind: "Above all, I bind the leadership of the nation and those under them to a meticulous observance of the racial laws and to merciless opposition to the universal poisoners of all peoples, international Jewry." The final solution of the "Jewish question," namely, the genocide of the Jewish race in Europe, takes on its proper significance as the final, logical product of Hitler's racial ideology. Once the Jew was purged from Europe, Germany would be able to produce pure Aryans who would be physically and spiritually perfect human beings. And thus Hitler's new order would be established with spiritually pure Aryans, demigod rulers, who, as Hitler enigmatically expressed it, "having achieved possession of this earth, will have a free path for activity in domains which will lie partly above it and partly outside it." 78 This last statement is a reminder that Hitler suggested on occasion that there was a deeper, cosmic significance to his new order. "National Socialism," he once exclaimed to Otto Strasser, "would be worth nothing if it were restricted merely to Germany and did not seal the supremacy of the superior Race over the entire world for at least a thousand to two thousand years."79 Even in Mein Kampf, Hitler hinted that such a master race would have to make "the last and greatest decisions on this earth." 80 Are these statements the fanciful flights of words of one who was accustomed to lack of proportion and moderation? Or are they the reflection of some of the sources that influenced the development of Hitler's ideas on racial ideology?

So much has been written about the sources for Hitler's racial ideology and other ideas that the standard histories of the Third Reich and the numerous biographies of Adolf Hitler seem content to repeat a well established litany of people and movements that may have influenced Hitler's thought. Indeed, the composer Richard Wagner, the philosophers Friedrich Nietzsche and Arthur Schopenhauer, the Viennese politicians George von Schonerer and Karl Lueger, the racial philosophers Joseph Arthur Gobineau and Houston Stewart

Chamberlain, extreme nationalism, Social Darwinism, and racism in general are all regularly cited as his main sources. 81 Since Hitler rarely specified his sources, scholars have resorted to indicating similarities and parallels in order to document these influences. The suggestion made in the 1950s by Joachim Besser and in the early 1960s by George Mosse that an examination of the impact of occult or esoteric philosophies, especially current in Vienna and Munich in the late nineteenth and early twentieth centuries, on Hitler and early National Socialism might indeed be a more fruitful line of approach to the problem, has not been widely pursued by academic historians. 82 Recently, however,

Jeffrey Goldstein and James Webb have emphasized the importance of occultism in general in the emergence of Nazi ideology. We would like to argue that occult or esoteric racial philosophy may, indeed, have been one of the major sources for Hitler's racial ideology. 83

Hitler himself may have been partly responsible for leading historians away from investigating esoteric influences. 84 It is well known that Hitler criticized occultists, Freemasons, and astrologers and even persecuted some of them when he came into power. And yet, in his nightly monologues to his assembled guests, Hitler revealed his belief in the very ideas that these groups were perpetrating. Ample evidence of this is provided in his references to reincarnation, the lost continent of Atlantis, and Hans Horbiger's world ice theory, as well as in his conviction that the early myths and legends of cosmic disasters and struggles between giants and gods are actually mankind's vague memory of a disaster that destroyed a humanity that already possessed an advanced degree of civilization. 85

A large variety of occult or esoteric groups and philosophies existed in German-speaking lands from the 1890s into the 1920s. One of the most influential schools of thought came out of the work established by the Russian Helena Blavatsky.86 Blavatsky, who had immersed herself deeply in esoteric spiritual beliefs from all over the world, formed a universal esoteric philosophy which she called Theosophy (Wisdom of the Gods). She viewed it as the revival of an ancient, occult knowledge derived from an earlier, advanced civilization which had known a unity between science and religion. In 1875, Blavatsky and Colonel Henry Olcott founded the Theosophical Society in New York City. Its purpose was to collect and diffuse this previously secret knowledge of the laws governing the universe. After the establishment of the first Theosophic lodge in 1884 in Germany, the movement spread rapidly in that country. In her esoteric work, especially The Secret Doctrine, originally published in 1888, Blavatsky emphasized the concept of races as paramount in the development of human history. According to Blavatsky, there are seven root races of mankind, with each root race containing seven sub-races. The present root race is the fifth, the Aryan, and was preceded by the fourth or Atlantean race. The Aryans evolved from the fifth sub-race of the Atlanteans. According to Blavatsky, "The Aryan Race was born and developed in the far North, though after the sinking of the Continent of Atlantis its tribes emigrated further south into Asia." 87 The Aryans, following a migratory pattern that went south and west from Asia, ultimately created the great Hindu, Persian, Greco-Roman, and later European cultures. Hitler, like his party ideologist, Alfred Rosenberg, also claimed Aryan origins for all of these cultures. 88

Each root race is seen by Blavatsky as being constituted differently in a physical and spiritual sense. In the earliest times man was purely spirit. Then at some point in time, this spirit entered and animated physical matter. Man thus evolved, in Blavatsky's cosmology, from the ethereal to the material. The original spirituality of man can be seen, according to Blavatsky, in the fact that mankind once was endowed with psychic powers, which she attributed to the so-called "Cyclopean eye."89 With the "Cyclopean eye" man had "spiritual sight," the ability to perceive subtle realities of the spiritual world, and thus could "see" into the future and read minds. Blavatsky felt that as man evolved materially and intellectually this "Third Eye" atrophied to what is now the pineal gland and man mostly lost his psychic powers.90 But, stated Blavatsky, mankind is destined to regain these abilities. That Hitler was well versed in these racial peculiarities is demonstrated in one of Herman Rauschning's conversations with Hitler:

> The pursuit of the "random path of the intelligence," we learned, was the real defection of man from his divine mission. To have "magic insight" was apparently Hitler's idea of the goal of human progress. He himself felt that he already had the rudiments of this gift. He attributed to it his success and his future eminence. A savant of Munich . . . had also written some curious stuff about the prehistoric world . . . about forms of perception and supernatural powers. There was the eye of Cyclops, or median eye, the organ of magic perception of the Infinite, now reduced to a rudimentary pineal gland. Speculations of this sort fascinated Hitler, and he would sometimes be entirely wrapped up in them. He saw his own remarkable career as a confirmation of hidden powers. He saw himself as chosen for superhuman tasks, as the prophet of the rebirth of man in a new form. 91

Might this "new form" of man of Hitler's be related to Blavatsky's root race schema? She maintained that the sixth and seventh root races would witness a return to the earlier spiritual state of existence. Man would once again have spiritual insight and be at one with the forces of nature. According to Hitler, "Creation is not yet at an end. . . . Man has clearly arrived at a turning point. . . . A new variety of man is beginning to separate out." Hitler further believed that mankind would evolve into two distinct types. "The two types will rapidly diverge from one another. One will sink to a sub-human race and the other rise far above the man of today. I might call the two varieties the god-man and the mass-animal." The new, godlike Aryan would rule over the inferior races, the "mass-animal." 92 To Hitler, it was the divine mission of the Nazi movement to bring this about: "Those who see in National Socialism nothing more than a political movement know scarcely anything of it. It is more even than a religion: it is the will to create mankind anew." 93 To accomplish this Hitler believed that the Nazi movement must return the Aryan to his original state, for example, oneness with Volk, "herd instinct," racial purity, and inner spirituality. If the Nazi movement was to lead the Aryan race back to its purest form, it must, Hitler felt, eliminate those factors that caused it to stray in the first place. These are the intellect, egoism, materialism, and impurity of blood. The existence of these elements was not, in Hitler's mind, an accident of Aryan evolution, but the result of the conspiratorial actions of the Jew.

It is important to observe that there are also some striking differences between Blavatsky's doctrine and Hitler's later racial ideas. Blavatsky herself did not identify the Aryan race with the Germanic peoples. And although her racial doctrine clearly entailed belief in superior and inferior races and hence could be easily misused, she placed no emphasis on the domination of one race over another. She certainly did not advocate the use of force since human racial evolution was an inevitable process that operated primarily on the basis of spiritual laws. Nevertheless, in her work Blavatsky had helped to foster antisemitism, which is perhaps one of the reasons her esoteric work was so rapidly accepted in German circles. She sharply differentiated Aryan and Jewish religion. The Aryans were the most spiritual people on earth. For them, religion was an "everlasting lodestar." For the Jews, religion was grounded on "mere calculation." They had a "religion of hate and malice toward everyone and everything outside itself." 94 Jewish materialism and selfishness contrasted strongly with Aryan spirituality and selflessness. This dualism is dramatically echoed in Hitler in the following passage:

> Two worlds face one another-the men of God and the men of Satan. The Jew is the anti-man, the creature of another god. He must have come from another root of the human race. I set the Aryan and the Jew over against each other; and if I call one of them a human being I must call the other something else. The two are as widely separated as man and beast. Not that I would call the Jew a beast. He is much further from the beasts than we Aryans. He is a creature outside nature and alien to nature.

Hitler's dualism, unlike Blavatsky's, was conceived simply as a conflict between two races: "The struggle for world domination will be fought entirely between us, between Germans and Jews." 95 If we regard these parallels between Blavatsky's esoteric thought and Hitler's racial ideology as significant, then we need to consider an additional question. What were the specific channels by which Theosophy reached or influenced Hitler? The occult revival in Germany and in Europe in general in the late nineteenth and early twentieth centuries led to a remarkable growth of Theosophic lodges as well as other occult groups.96 But in Germany Theosophical speculation, especially on race and nature mysticism, became combined with volkisch movements that were nationalistic and antisemitic. The resulting combination of occultism, volkisch nationalism, racism, and antisernitism became known in Germany as Ariosophy. It is possible that Ariosophy provides the link between Theosophy and Hitler's racial ideology.

The leading figures of Ariosophy were two Austrian occultists, Guido von List and Lanz von Liebenfels. Guido von List (1848–1919) was a free-lance author who turned increasingly to mystical and occult themes in his writings. His supporters formed the Guido von List Society in Vienna in 1903. It soon became one of the leading Viennese occult groups. Its members included the well-known Theosophist Franz Hartmann, the chief of staff of the Austro-Hungarian army, wealthy merchants in Vienna and Germany, and the affluent Munich industrialist Friedrich Wannieck, who largely financed the society. The primary purpose of the society was to circulate and perpetuate the books and ideas of List. 97 List's ideas were explicated in a series of occult books. In Die Religio der Ario-Germanen (The Religion of the Ario-Germans) List established the fundamental beliefs of Ariosophy. There is a life-force that pervades the universe and its mysteries could be grasped solely by people closely in tune with nature. Only the Ario-Germans were capable of this attunement since they were the most removed from modem rationalistic and materialistic society. The Jews, on the other hand, were viewed as a prime example of lower races since they were heavily involved in rationalism and materialism. In his work Die Armanenschaft der Ario-Germanen (The Armanen Caste of the ArioGermans) List made proposals for an Ario-Germanic state. It would be based on the recognition of the superiority of Aryan peoples and the need for lower races to serve the higher race. Only Ario-Germans could hold leadership positions in the state, schools, professions, industry and banks, newspapers, theater and the arts. Racial laws would maintain the purity of the Ario-Germanic race by prohibiting racial intermarriage and by reserving citizenship for Ario- Germans. A new school system based on levels would reserve the highest level for the "Armanen," the Aryan leaders who were distinguished by their ability to use the occult powers of the soul to know the secrets of the ancient wisdom-religion. 98 The parallels of List's Ario-Germanic state to Hitler's Nazi state are indeed striking.

List was also interested in occult signs and symbols. In Das Geheimnis der Runen (The Secret of the Runes) he portrayed runes as the sacred symbols of ancient Aryan knowledge which, interpreted properly, could provide a real understanding of spiritual forces. He used the swastika, which he depicted as a fundamental occult symbol of salvation, to represent the victory of the Aryans over the lower races. Blavatsky had also considered the swastika as a powerful occult symbol and had used it in the seal of the Theosophical Society.99 in Mein Kampf Hitler had viewed the swastika as symbolizing " . . . the mission of the struggle for the victory of the Aryan man, and . . . the victory of the idea of creative work, which as such always has been and always will be anti-Semitic."100 There can be little doubt about the close relationship between List's Ariosophy and Theosophy. Franz Hartmann, himself a prominent Theosophist, explained how List's teachings, especially on racial doctrine bore remarkable resemblance to those of Blavatsky. The kinship between List's Ariosophy and Theosophy is also especially noticeable in Prana, a German occult monthly for applied spiritualism. It was published by the Theosophical publishing house at Leipzig and edited by Johannes Baltzli, a Theosophist who was secretary of the Guido von List Society and biographer of List. Contributors to Prana included the Theosophists Franz Hartmann and C.W. Leadbeater, and Guido von List himself. The journal's name represented the power of the sun, considered the visible symbol of God. Prana emphasized the importance of vegetarianism. It argued that the eating of meat impeded the ability to understand nature and hence the cosmic life-force. Alcohol was thought to have the same negative qualities.54 It is interesting to note that Hitler became both a dedicated vegetarian and teetotaler by the 1920s.

Whether Hitler had a direct, personal relationship to the Guido von List Society during his years in Vienna from 1907–1913 has not been definitively established. The List Society was certainly prominent in the occult circles that stressed volkisch nationalism and antisernitism. And Hitler did emphasize in Mein Kampf that in Vienna he established "a world picture and a philosophy which became the granite foundation" of all his actions.101 That "granite foundation" was centered in his racial ideology. Nevertheless, it is more probable that Hitler did come into direct contact with another major proponent of Ariosophy in Vienna, Lanz von Liebenfels. Lanz von Liebenfels (1874–1954) moved from Catholic monasticism to an involvement in occultism, racism, and German nationalism. He came to characterize his occupation as "racial researcher, philosopher of religion and sexual mystic," all of which were consonant with various forms of occultism. He founded a quasi-religious Order of the New Templars whose primary purpose was to foster Ariosophical doctrines. He established his first New Templars castle in the Burg Werfenstein on the Danube in 1907 and proudly flew a swastika flag over it. By the 1920s he had established three more castles and a house in Salzburg as part of his Templar movement. He served as a member of the board of directors of the Guido von List Society. 102

Lanz von Liebenfels wrote a series of occult works that presented his Ariosophical philosophy, although his major work Theozoologie (Theo- zoology), written in 1904, contains the essence of his thought. That philosophy, like List's, was based on the superiority of the Ario-Germans. The Aryan was an exalted spiritual being: "The Aryan hero is on this planet the most complete incarnation of God and of the Spirit." Jews, as well as other inferior races, were characterized as "animal- men" who must someday be eliminated by genetic selection, sterilization, deportations, forced labor, and even "direct liquidation." The elimination of the "animal-man" made possible the coming of the "higher new man." Liebenfels also propagated his occult racial views in a magazine called Ostara and subtitled "Library of Those Who are Blond and Defend the Rights of the Male." 103 According to Liebenfels, there was a close affinity between Theosophy and his brand of Ariosophy.

In discussing Blavatsky's work, The Secret Doctrine, he wrote enthusiastically that "she was almost a generation ahead of her time and of anthropology. Today for the first time work on the latest material has brought to light results which show a completely amazing identity with those of the spiritual Theosophist." It was claimed by a friend that Lanz had direct contact with Blavatsky and her immediate successor as head of the Theosophical movement, Annie Besant. 104

The direct impact of Lanz von Liebenfels on Hitler is by no means accepted by all historians. However, Liebenfels claimed that he had personal contact with Hitler when the future Führer visited him in 1909 to obtain some back issues of Ostara. 105 The New Templar movement was still active during the growth of the Nazi party and Liebenfels himself made several direct assertions concerning the close relationship of his movement to Hitler's. He wrote in 1925: Already there appear the outlines of a new Ariosophical, Ario-Christian International: Fascism in Italy, Awakening Hungary, the Spanish Fascists, the North American Ku Klux Man and finally the Swastikamovement in Germany, directly proceeding from Ariosophy. In 1932 Liebenfels wrote to one of his New Templar brothers: "Do you know that Hitler is one of our pupils? You will still live to see that he, and thereby we, also will triumph and kindle a movement that will make the world tremble." 106 Are these statements pure fantasy? Or did Liebenfels know of Hitler's affinity to his movement?

Without new evidence it may be impossible to prove to everyone's satisfaction that Hitler was directly influenced in the development of his racial ideology by Guido von List and Lanz von Liebenfels. But there can be little doubt, based on the parallels found in Hitler and in both Theosophy and Ariosophy that the occult climate of Vienna in Hitler's "formative years" did have an impact on him. Hitler experienced a similar environment after the war when he returned to Munich. Postwar Germany, as one contemporary noted, was rife with occultism:

> Germany seems to be gripped by an occult fever. Its victims are like drug-addicts; every new psychic fashion claims thousands of adherents and dozens of victims. . . . Men and women have become exhausted by the sorrows and horrors of reality; they flee to the world of imagination; the maze of everyday life enfolds them and they hope to find a way out through occultism and dreams. 65

The Bavarian capital of Munich was likewise a scene of much occult activity and Hitler had ample opportunity to experience it. In the conversation with Rauschning quoted earlier in this paper, Hitler refers to his knowledge of a Munich occultist who had written about the "Cyclopean eye." 107 As a frequent visitor at the home of Hugo and Elsa Bruckmann in 1922 and 1923, Hitler probably heard some of the lectures of Alfred Schuler, a disciple of Guido von List. Most important, however, Hitler associated with various members of the Thule Society, an occult society that combined occult racial philosophy with a belief in militant action. Ariosophy, like Theosophy, had relied on intellectual expositions of racial evolution. The Thule Society preached Aryan supremacy and acted to achieve it. It provides the final link between occult racial theories and the racial ideology of Hitler and the emerging Nazi party. The Thule Society was basically a continuation of the Germanen Order, whose first lodge was established in Berlin in 1912. Modeled after the organization of Freemasonry, the aims of the Germanen Order were to achieve German racial purity, attack the Jews, and establish Germans as the leaders of Europe. In 1917, Rudolf von Sebottendorf was made head of the Order's Bavarian province. In order to provide a cover for the Order's activities, he founded the Thule Society in January 1918. The Thule Society functioned outwardly as a "German Studies" group. Despite its outer appearance, it was actively involved in the counter-revolutionary forces against the Bavarian Soviet Republic, which the Thule felt was dominated by Jews. 108

It was Thule people to whom Hitler first came and it was Thule people who first united themselves with Hitler. The armament of the coming Führer consisted, besides the Thule itself, of the German Workers' Society, founded in the Thule Society by brother Karl Harrer and the German-Socialist Party led by Hans Georg Grassinger, whose organ was the Munchener Beobachter, later the Volkische Beobachter. From these three sources Hitler created the National Socialist German Worker's Party. 109 Undoubtedly, Sebottendorf exaggerated his own significance.70 There is no evidence that he and Hitler ever met. Nevertheless, the German Worker's Party, which Hitler joined and later renamed, was founded by Anton Drexler early in 1919 under the chairmanship of Karl Harrer, a member of the Thule. In fact, the German Workers' Party had a number of close links with the Thule society. Hitler also had intimate ties with Thule members. Dietrich Eckart, whom Hitler accepted as his mentor and praised as the original father of the Nazi movement, Alfred Rosenberg, eventually the Nazi party's ideologist, and Rudolf Hess, Hitler's future second-in-command, were all members of the Thule Society. Sebottendorf's Thule Society, with its occult, racist ideas is, regardless of any exaggeration in Sebottendorf's claims, connected to the beginning of Hitler's National Socialism.

Significantly, the Thule Society was well grounded in occultist philosophy. Eckart, Rosenberg, and Hess shared occult interests. In his writings, Dietrich Eckart combined German racism, his own version of occult Christian mysticism, and a profound knowledge of Theosophy and occultism in general. Alfred Rosenberg, an intimate of Eckart, shared his mystical preoccupations. In his work, The Myth of the Twentieth Century, he developed an "occult history" of mankind based on the lost Atlantis. Rudolf Hess was especially interested in astrology and astrological prophecies and herbalist lore founded upon the occult "doctrine of correspondences." Thule's founder Rudolf von Sebottendorf was a practicing occultist. He wrote a history of Turkish Freemasonry and a history of astrology that was really a discussion of occult prehistory. He edited an astrological magazine and another called Runen, which was decorated with swastikas. 110 According to Sebottendorf himself, the Germanen Order and Thule Society were basically dependent for their intellectual foundation on Guido von List and Lanz von Liebenfels. Indeed, the connection of the Thule Society to Ariosophy is evident in a headline of Thule's newspaper, the Mfinchener Beobachter. It read "Down with the Tschandalen," the latter being Liebenfels's name for the inferior races who faced liquidation. 111

Our examination of the Ariosophy of Guido von List and Lanz von Liebenfels and the Thule Society described the possible channels by which Theosophical thought might have reached Hitler and helped to determine his own racial ideology. Considerably more research remains to be done to show specifically how Hitler and other Nazis came into direct contact with esoteric philosophy and more important, what the ramifications of this new information are. The lack of originality in Hitler's thought is apparent. But Hitler's true originality was his ability to translate ideas into reality. His racial ideology, derived in part from perversion of esoteric thought, did, after all, become racial genocide.

Chapter Seven

The State and Violence

NAZI PARTY ORGANIZATION BOOK (1940)

The following extracts are taken from the Nazi Party Organization Book (1940) and illustrate the duties of party members, as well as the National Socialist concept of the State:

6. Duties of the Party Comrade
The National Socialist commandments:
The Führer is always right!
Never go against discipline!
Don't waste your time in idle chatter or in self-satisfying criticism, but take hold and do your work!
Be proud but not arrogant!
Let the program be your dogma. It demands of you the greatest devotion to the movement.
You are a representative of the party; control your bearing and your manner accordingly!
Let loyalty and unselfishness be your highest precepts!
Practice true comradeship and you will be a true socialist!
Treat your racial comrades as you wish to be treated by them!
In battle be hard and silent!
Spirit is not unruliness!
That which promotes the movement, Germany, and your people, is right!
If you act according to these commandments, you are a true soldier of your Führer.

7. Guiding Principles for Members of the Ortsgruppen [local groups]

The following guiding principles are to be made known to all members, and all men and women of the party should impress them upon themselves:

Lighten the work of the political leaders by the punctual performance of your duties.

Women of the party should participate in the activities of the NS Association of Women there they will find work to do.

Don't buy from Jews!

Spare the health of the party comrades and speakers and refrain voluntarily from smoking at the meetings.

Don't make yourself a mouthpiece for our political opponents by spreading false reports.

To be a National Socialist is to set an example.

I. The State

The state is born out of the necessity of ordering the community of the Volk in accordance with certain laws. Its characteristic attribute is power over every branch of the community. The state has the right to demand of every racial comrade [Volksgenosse] that he live according to the law. Whoever violates the laws of the state will be punished. The state has officials to execute its laws and regulations. The constitution of the state is the basis for its legislation. The state embodies power! In the state men of different opinions and different outlook can live beside each other. The state cannot demand that all men be of the same opinion. It can, however, demand that all men observe its laws.

II. The Party

In contrast to the state, the party is the community of men of like opinion. It is born out of the struggle for an ideology. In order to survive this struggle, it gathered together all men who were prepared to fight for this ideology. The ideology is the basis of the order in accordance with which men live within the party. While in the state laws are considered as pressure, obstacles, and difficulties by many citizens, the laws of the party are no burden but rather signify the will of the community. In the state the characteristic is the must; in the party the I will.

III. The Functions of the Party and the State

(a) It is conceivable that party and state are one and the same thing. This is the case when all racial comrades are converted to the ideology of the party and the laws of the state are the clear expression of the will of the ideology. Then the state becomes the great community of men of like opinion. This ideal situation will only seldom be attained in history. It is, in fact, only conceivable if this ideology is the only basis for the inner attitude and takes complete possession of the people. . . .

(c) If the Volk in all its branches is not impregnated by the party and its ideology, party and state must remain separated. The party will then be an order in which a select group of leaders and fighters is found. The ideology will be carried to the Volk by these fighters. The party shall prepare public opinion and public desire so that the spiritual condition of the Volk shall be in accord with the actual legislation of the state.

Therefore it does not suffice for the party to be an elite, a minority which is bound together in unity. The party has rather the task of accomplishing the political education and the political unification of the German Volk. It accordingly is charged also with the leadership of its associated organizations. In the course of this leadership the party fulfills its primary task: the ideological conquest of the German Volk and the creation of the "Organization of the Volk." The state is a technical instrument to assist in the creation of this community of the people. It is the instrument for the realization of the ideology. The party is, therefore, the primary which constantly refills dead material with life and the will to life.

The state administrative apparatus functioned before the war and functioned also after the war. Notwithstanding, the German Volk experienced the Black Day of November 9, 1918; notwithstanding, it experienced the terrible collapse of the post war period in all fields of political, cultural, and economic life. Germany could only be saved from sinking into Communistic chaos through the spirit, will, and readiness to sacrifice of the German freedom movement. Its forces of will and spirit alone made reconstruction possible. The party now has the right and the task of again pumping streams of its spirit and will into the state apparatus. (8)

AYRIAN SELF-SACRIFICE

We think of National Socialism as the quintessence of brutality and immorality. The Nazis did not see it this way. Goebbels stated that to be a National Socialist meant to "subordinate the I to the Thou, sacrifice the personality for the whole." He defined Nazism as "service, renunciation for individuals and a claim for the whole, fanatic of love, courage to sacrifice, resignation for the Volk." A U.S. Department of State booklet explicated Nazi ideology as a conviction that "consecrates its whole life to the service of an idea, a faith, a task or duty even when it knows that the destruction of its own life is certain." Goebbels contrasted the creative, constructive philosophy of National Socialism with its idealistic goals to the Jewish philosophy of "materialism and individualism." Hitler's Official Programme published in 1927 inveighed against the leaders of public life who all worshipped the same god, "individualism," and whose sole incentive was "personal interest." The essence of the Nazi complaint was that the Jew lacked the capacity to sacrifice himself in the name of the community.

The popular concept is that the Nazis were intent upon producing a race of "supermen." Hitler did believe in the "superiority" of the Aryan race, but his idea of what constituted Aryan superiority is quite different than what is commonly assumed. Further, what made Aryans superior did not necessarily guarantee victory in war. On the contrary, Hitler feared, the Aryan trait that made them superior as culture-builders might lead to the downfall and extinction of the race rather than to its triumph and survival. According to Hitler's theory propounded in Mein Kampf, what was unique about the Aryan was his willingness to abandon self-interest and transcend egoism in the name of surrendering to the community. What was "most strongly developed in the Aryan," Hitler said, was the "self-sacrificing will to give one's personal labor and if necessary one's own life for others." The Aryan was "not greatest in his mental abilities as such," but rather in the "extent of his willingness to put all his abilities in the service of the community." The Aryan according to Hitler willingly "subordinates his own ego to the life of the community" and "if the hour demands it" even sacrifices himself. The Jew by contrast, Hitler said, represented the "mightiest counterpart to the Aryan." Whereas the Aryan willingly sacrificed himself for the community, in the Jewish people the "will to self-sacrifice does not go beyond the individual's naked instinct of self-preservation." The Jew lacked completely, Hitler believed, the "most essential requirement for a cultured people, the idealistic attitude." The Jew's "absolute absence of all sense of sacrifice" expressed itself as "cowardice."

HITLER AND WORLD WAR ONE

Hitler was one of the sixty-five million men who fought in the First World War; an instance of mass-slaughter in which nine-million men were killed and nearly thirty million wounded or reported missing. During the period of 1914–1918 across Europe and the wider world men were killed at an average rate of more than six thousand per day. Hitler was among those who suffered in the trenches, endured the wet and the cold and the scarcity of food, the rats and bedbugs, and the endless artillery barrage. He witnessed the death and dismemberment of hundreds of his comrades and experienced the stench of their decaying bodies. It is miraculous that Hitler himself was not killed. According to Walter S. Frank's study of Hitler and the First World War, the chance that a 1914 volunteer in Hitler's regiment would be killed or maimed was almost guaranteed. Because of replacements, Hitler's regiment, which consisted of 3600 men in 1914, suffered 3754 killed before the war ended. Hitler told an English reporter that on one occasion while eating, he moved from one spot in a trench to another twenty yards away. Only a few seconds later, an artillery shell exploded on the very spot from which he had moved, killing every one of his comrades. Hitler was temporarily blinded by poison gas and lying in a hospital bed when the war ended in 1918. 31

One might expect that Hitler's trench experiences would have humanized, sensitized him to the suffering and destruction wrought by war. One would think that he would have become highly critical of the leaders of his nation's war effort such as von Hindenburg and Ludendorff whose military strategies led to the deaths of two million German soldiers. Yet astonishingly Hitler rarely complained or expressed regrets about what he had gone through. Nor did he cease to admire and support Germany 's military leaders.

Why can't human beings abandon war, which is the source of profound suffering, degradation and death? Why did Hitler's experiences not lead him to critique the institution of warfare? The problem is that the idea of war is bound to the ideology of nationalism. People can be persuaded to fight and die because they are deeply attached and feel obligated to their own nations. In Mein Kampf, Hitler wrote: "When in the long war years Death snatched so many a dear comrade and friend from our ranks, it would have seemed to me almost a sin to complain. After all, were they not dying for Germany?" Hitler asserted that "Any man who loves his people proves it solely by the sacrifices which he is prepared to make for it." He stated that National Socialism meant acting with a "boundless and all embracing love for the people, and if necessary to die for it." He proclaimed that giving one's life for the community constituted the "crown of all sacrifice." The apogee of love and devotion within the framework of Hitler's radical nationalism was the willingness to die for one's country. Nazism was an ideology of martyrdom revolving around "laying down one's life for one's people and country." 34

What had been the purpose of the war? Why had two million German soldiers been killed and four million wounded? What had been the meaning of the monumental sacrifices? These questions cried out for an answer. Hitler responded to the question of the meaning of German sacrifices by deflecting it with another one. The question, "Why had Germans soldiers died?" transmogrified into the question, "Why had German soldiers died while other Germans had not died." Hitler observed that for each "Hero who had made the supreme sacrifice" there was a "shirker who cunningly dodged death." Hitler became obsessed with the idea that while so many men had died, others had avoided fighting altogether. Contemplating the idea that many had sacrificed their lives while others had not, Hitler became deeply disturbed and enraged.

We have observed that Hitler judged the worth of a human being on the basis of his capacity for sacrifice. He stated that during the First World War "one extreme of the population, which was constituted of the best elements, had given a typical example of its heroism and had sacrificed itself almost to a man;" whereas "the other extreme, which was constituted of the worst elements of the population, had preserved itself almost intact." While for four and a half years our "best human material was being thinned to an exceptional degree on the battlefields," the worst material "wonderfully succeeded in saving themselves." 42

Thus a conundrum arose that would preoccupy Hitler throughout his life: Why in war do the best human beings die while the worst survive? Our ordinary expectation is that if we perform in accordance with morality or virtue, we will be rewarded; whereas if we act immorally, we will be punished. Yet Hitler discovered that what occurs in war acts in opposition to what we feel should occur. In war, those who adhere to societal norms by enthusiastically performing their duty are killed. While those who behave immorally by evading their responsibility to society survive. Hitler was alarmed and agitated by the profound unfairness or injustice of this state of affairs.

SACRIFICIAL DEATH

As the attack against Russia began, German General von Rundstedt admonished the soldier of the Second World War to emulate the examples of his brothers in the First World War and "to die in the same way, to be as strong, unswerving and obedient, to go happily and as a matter of course to his death." As war on the Eastern Front progressed, Goebbels was satisfied to note that "The German soldiers go into battle with devotion, like congregations going into service." German soldiers did not rebel against the duty to fight and die. They went like sheep to the slaughter. 46 Hitler joined the army in 1914 at the behest of his nation and its leaders. In 1939 twenty-five years later, he was Germany's leader. Now it was his turn to declare war and to ask young men to enter the battlefield. Hitler's familiarity with war did not deter him. He knew that Germany's soldiers would die and be maimed. However, now that he was Germany's leader and commander-in-chief, why should he waver? Had the German leadership hesitated to declare war in 1914 and to send his comrades and him to die at the front? Was a soldier not obligated to do his duty, to fight when asked by his nation to do so and if necessary to make the 'supreme sacrifice'?

JEWISH SACRIFICE

The Final Solution or systematic extermination of the Jewish people began before the construction of death camps and gas chambers. As the German army moved eastward into the Soviet Union in late 1941 and early 1942, they were followed by the Einsatzgruppen or mobile killing units. Millions of Jews were shot and killed, many of them buried in gorges that bear a striking re-

semblance to the trenches of the First World War. Hitler professed to be
undisturbed by the extermination of men, women, and children, providing the
following rationale: "If I don't mind sending the pick of the German people
into the hell of war without regret for the shedding of valuable German blood
then I have naturally the right to destroy millions of men of inferior races who
increase like vermin." 29

Here we approach the crux of the matter and the meaning of the Holocaust.
Hitler appears to be saying that if he had no compunctions about sending German soldiers to die in battle, then why should he have any compunctions
about sending Jews—mortal enemies of the German people—to their deaths?
The logic of genocide derived from the logic of war. Hitler declared that if
German soldiers had to die, so must Jews. No one could be exempt. Everyone would be required to sacrifice their lives for Germany. What disturbed
Hitler about the First World War was his belief that some had died whereas
others had not; that the best had been killed whereas the worst had survived.
Hitler was enraged when he contemplated the idea that many Germans had
sacrificed their lives, while others—shirkers, war deserters, and Jews—had
avoided fighting entirely. In this second war, Hitler insisted, things would be
different. This time, everyone would participate equally. Even Jews would lay
down their lives.

Ronald Hayman in his biographical study of Hitler reports an encounter between Hitler and his friend Henny von Schirach. She had returned to Germany in April 1943 after she had visited friends in occupied Amsterdam and
became aware that helpless women were being taken away and transported to
camps. After dinner at Obersalzberg, Hitler turned to his friend and said
"You've come from Holland?" She replied, "Yes, that's why I'm here, I
wanted to talk to you. I've seen frightful things. I can't believe that's what
you want." "You're sentimental, Frau von Schirach," Hitler replied. Then he
jumped to his feet and formed with his hands two bowls which he moved up
and down like scales as he said loudly and insistently:

Look—every day ten thousand of my most valuable men are killed, men who
are irreplaceable, the best. The balance is wrong; the equilibrium in Europe has
been upset. Because the others aren't being killed. They survive, the ones in
camps, the inferior ones. So what's it going to look like in Europe in a hundred
years? In a thousand? Hitler undertook the extermination of the Jews, this passage suggests, in order to balance the scale of death. As the best human beings—
German soldiers—were dying in vast numbers on the field of battle, so it would
be necessary to make certain that the worst human beings—Jews—died as well.
Members of the Aryan race, loyal and obedient, would willingly sacrifice their
lives. The German soldier, as General von Runstedt put it, would go "happily
and as a matter of course to his death." He would be prepared at any moment as

Hitler stated in his declaration of war to "lay down his life for his people and his country." Jews on the other hand, according to Hitler, were a race that was incapable or unwilling to sacrifice for the community. In the case of the Jew, therefore, it was necessary that he be compelled to die. 10

Holocaust

THE HOLOCAUST: SACRIFICIAL DEATH STRIPPED OF HONOR, HEROISM AND GLORY

The Second World War and the Holocaust were two sides of the same coin. War provided for Hitler the occasion to sacrifice his own people. Once again the German soldier would demonstrate his "loyalty and obedience unto death." The Holocaust represented another form or manifestation of "dying for the country." The norms of war define soldiers—one's own and the enemy's—as the class of people that are responsible for dying. Genocide constituted an extension of the logic of war, enlarging the pool of sacrificial victims.

Historians speak of Hitler's extermination of the Jews as the Holocaust. The word derives from the word olah in the Hebrew Bible. It had the religious meaning of a burnt-sacrifice. In the Greek translation of the Old Testament the word became holokauston. The English definition made it "an offering wholly consumed by fire." What Hitler did added another meaning to the dictionary definition: "A complete or thorough sacrifice or destruction, especially by fire, as of large number of human beings." 31

Use of the term Holocaust to describe what occurred suggests that we do understand that the extermination of the Jews constituted a sacrifice. However, we have hesitated to articulate the precise meaning of this sacrifice, perhaps because even now we do not wish to acknowledge that with regard to the fate of the Jews, Hitler accomplished what he set out to achieve. In the Holocaust, Hitler sacrificed the Jewish people to the god that he worshipped, Germany.

In the First World War, German soldiers had sacrificed themselves in massive numbers. Hitler felt that Jews had acted deviously in order to avoid fighting and dying. In the Second World War, German soldiers again would be expected to "lay down their lives for their people and country" (as Hitler put it in his Declaration of War). In this war, however, unlike the first one, Hitler insisted that Jews would not be allowed to be "shirkers". Hitler stated in his Declaration of War that if anyone thought that he could "evade the national duty" (to lay down one's life for the country), that person would "perish." The Final Solution was undertaken to make certain that Jews—like German soldiers—would give their bodies over to the nation-state and die when asked to do so.

The Holocaust reveals the abject and degrading fate of a body that has been given over to, taken over by the state. A soldier is required to enter into battle at the behest of his nation. Often, he dies a brutal, ugly and horrific death. However, in spite of the brutality and ugliness of his death, the soldier's sacrifice—dying for his country—frequently has been viewed as noble and beautiful. It is impossible, on the other hand, to view the death of a Jew in the gas chamber as noble and beautiful. The Holocaust depicts the ugliness, futility and meaninglessness of submission to the nation state, sacrificial death stripped of words such as honor, heroism and glory. 40

Violence

The Nazis held struggle and violence to be an irreducible first principle of life "which is neither derived nor in need of proof" a basic conditioned of all nature and the basis for all higher development. The phrase that war is life was often repeated, that war is the father of all things, that life is struggle, that nature is an arena of perpetual struggle, that only force rules, compelling the victory of the strong over the weak, that force is the first law. Those who want to live, let them fight, and those who do not want to fight in this world of eternal struggle do not deserve to live. Violence was the preferred exalted mode of behavior, the willingness to fight served as the highest criterion of worthiness for any individual, irrespective of all considerations of caution or personal safety. The mechanistic perfection of marching columns was meant to control apprehension about self and body, asserting the viability of life through order and providing a basis for mastery of the world. There was a constant dwelling among Nazis on the frontline experience, on the virtues of war, on the real anticipated confrontation with pain and death, with fantasies of unlimited accomplishment based on military prowess. The Nazis were constantly preoccupied with military adventures, meaning to establish their superiority through exploitation of the weakness of others, urging action as if there could be no realistic limitations to such action. One had to constantly prove "the right to exist" in never ending combat, the ideal being the farmer-warrior of the eastern reached in Hitler's imagination.

The emphasis on struggle and violence served a number of purposes, initially the mobilization of people to resist the humiliation of defeat and the fostering of a spirit of recovery and renewal in the face of a deprived and unjust reality. Hitler seamed to understand the feelings of humiliation, or fears of enforced passivity, are most forcefully mastered by injunctions against appearing shameful and contemptible, independent of any moral norm or obligation, as feelings aroused by fears of weakness, unworthiness, and shame are most compellingly controlled by action that confirms pride and superiority without any regard for its effect on others. The emphasis then also served as a means of encouraging people to realize a cherished ideal: combative masculine activity in a spirit of discipline and sacrifice. The idea was tied to a vulgar and inconsistent "Social Darwinsim", to ideas of race and blood, and of a menaced future, expressed in pseudoscientific and semi-scientific terms that permitted a "realistic" stress on the eternal laws of nature and fighting it out with brutal determination in an unyielding acceptance of the need continuously to fight for life, the voluntary sacrifice of all, and the merciless treatment of racial enemies. 111

References

1. Joachim Fest, The Face of the Third Reich, Penguin, Harmondsworth, Middlesex, 1963.

2. Paul Johnson, A History of the Modern World, Weidenfeld, London, 1983, pp. 104–138.

3. William Shirer, The Rise and Fall of the Third Reich, Pan, London, p. 129.

4. Henry Pachter, Weimar Etudes, Columbia University Press, New York, 1982, p. 266.

5. Nigel Pennick, Hitler's Secret Sciences, Neville Spearman, Sudbury, Suffolk, 1981, pp. 123–124.

6. Pachter, 1982, pp. 261–262.

7. Shirer, 1960, p. 130.

8. Pennick, 1981, p. 87.

9. Shirer, 1960, pp. 137–148.

10. Johnson, 1983, pp. 126–127.

11. Herman Glaser, The Cultural Roots of National Socialism, Croom Helm, London, 1978, p. 99.

12. George Mosse, The Germans and the Jews, Orbach and Chambers, London, 1971, pp. 37–51.

13. Johnson, 1983, p. 119.

14. Glaser, 1978, p. 224.

15. Mosse, 1971, p. 113.

16. This section ("The Lords of Unreason") draws widely on The Occult Roots of Nazism by Nicholas Goodrick Clarke (Wellingborough, 1985) one of the few books written which offers a rationalist examination of the relationship between the occult and National Socialism.

17. Shirer, 1960, p. 299.

18. Glaser, 1978, p. 102 and Pachter, 1982, p. 263.

19. Mosse, 1971, p. 155.

20. Robert Skidelsky, Oswald Mosley, Macmillan, London, 1975, p. 336–352.

21. As shown by the Sunday Times profile of David Icke (Sunday 31st March 1991), erstwhile chief spokesman of the Green Party.

22. Martin Broszat, German National Socialism, Santa Barbara, 1966.

23. Eberhard Jäckel, Hitler's Weltanschauung. A Blueprint for Power, Middletown, Connecticut, 1972.

24. Ian Kershaw, The 'Hitler Myth'. Image and Reality in the Third Reich, 2nd edn., Oxford, 2001.

25. Ian Kershaw, 'Ideology, Propaganda, and the Rise of the Nazi Party', in Peter D.

26. Stachura (ed.), The Nazi Machtergreifung, London, 1983.

27. B.M. Lane and L.J. Rupp, Nazi Ideology before 1933, Manchester, 1978.

28. P.H. Merkl, Political Violence under the Swastika, Princeton, 1975.

29. Edouard Calic, Secret Conversations with Hitler (New York, 1971), p. 68.

30. Adolf Hitler, Mein Kampf, trans. Ralph Manheim (Boston, 1943), p. 339.

31. Mein Kampf, pp. 327, 381 and especially 396 on blood and soul; also on God's role, see speech of 1937 in Gordon Prange, ed., Hitler's Words (Washington, DC, 1944), p. 80.

32. Mein Kampf, p. 394.

33. Ibid., p. 290.

34. Ibid., p. 383.

35. Ibid., p. 296; see also pp. 249, 286–89; and Hitler's notes for a "monumental world history" in Werner Maser, ed., Hitler's Letters and Notes (New York, 1974), p. 280.

36. Mein Kampf, p. 300.

37. Ibid., p. 306.

38. Ibid., p. 324; also see Maser, Hitler's Letters, p. 221, and Calic, Secret Conversations, p. 66.

39. Mein Kampf, pp. 316, 325.

40. Ibid., pp. 324, 326.

41. Ibid., pp. 91, 313, 316; especially on internationalism, see Hitler's speech of 1922 in Prange, Hitler's Words, pp. 73, 75–76; one of Hitler's most thorough arguments on the Jews' creation of democracy, liberalism, and parliaments is in a speech of 1922 in The Speeches of Adolf Hitler, 1922–1939, ed . Norman H. Baynes, 2 vols. (Oxford, 1942), vol. 1, pp. 23–24.

42. Mein Kampf, p. 382.

43. Ibid., pp. 393–94.

44. Ibid., pp. 65, 320, 325, 382, 447; see also Hitler's speech of 28 July 1922 in Prange, Hitler's Words, p. 73.

45. Mein Kampf, p. 382.

46. Ibid., pp. 383–84, 391, 398.

47. Ibid., pp. 397–98.

48. [bid., pp. 346, 380.

49. Ibid., pp. 351, 384.

50. Ibid., p. 338.

51. Ernst Deuerlein, "Hitlers Eintritt in die Politik und die Reichswehr," Vierteljahrshefte ffir Zeitgeschichte 7 (1959): 204.

52. Max Domarus, ed., Hitler: Reden und Proklamationen, 1932–1945, 2 vols. (Munich, 1962–1963), vol. 2, p. 2239.

53. Mein Kampf, pp. 383–84.

54. Baynes, Speeches of Adolf Hitler, vol. 1, p. 775.

55. Karl Dietrich Bracher, The German Dictatorship, trans. Jean Steinberg (New York, 1970), pp. 7–45, 50–57.

56. Alan Bullock, Hitler, A Study in Tyranny (New York, 1962), pp. 36–46, 374, 382–85, 397–408.

57. R.H. Samuels, "The Origin and Development of the Ideology of National Socialism," The Australian Journal of Politics and History 9 (May 1963): 59–77.

58. Joachim Besser, "Die Vorgeschichte des Nationalsozialismus im neuen Licht," Die Pforte 2, no. 21–22 (Nov. 1950): 768–85.

59. George Mosse, "The Mystical Origins of National Socialism," Journal of the History of Ideas 22 (Jan.-Mar. 1961): 81–96.

60. Jeffrey Goldstein, "On Racism and Anti-Semitism in Occultism and Nazism," Yad Vashem Studies 13 (1979): 53–72.

61. James Webb, The Occult Establishment (LaSalle, IL, 1976), especially pp. 21–79, 275–344.

62. Francis King, Satan and Swastika (St. Albans, 1976); pp. 14–51, 120–146.

63. J.H. Brennan, Occult Reich (New York, 1974); pp. 31–56.

64. Jean-Michel Angebert, The Occult and the Third Reich, trans. Lewis Sumberg (New York, 1974); pp. 2–18,

65. Hitler's Secret Conversations, 1941–1944, trans. Norman Cameron and R.H. Stevens (New York, 1953), pp. 33, 67, 118, 203–04, 263.

66. Marion Meade, Madame Blavatsky (New York, 1980), pp. 31–51.

67. Ibid., vol. 2, pp. 111, 278, 411, 527.

68. Alfred Rosenberg, Der Mythus des 20. jahrhunderts (Munich, 1934), pp. 21–

69. Blavatsky, Secret Doctrine, vol. 2, pp. 90–94.

70. Ibid., pp. 307, 313.

71. Ibid., pp. 302–16.

72. Hermann Rauschning, Hitler Speaks (London, 1939), p. 240.

73. Blavatsky, Secret Doctrine, vol. 2, pp. 339–94.

74. Rauschning, Hitler Speaks, p. 238.

75. Ibid., p. 234.

76. Besser, "Die Vorgeschichte des Nationalsozialismus im. neuen Licht," pp. 770–72.

77. Baltzli, Guido von List, pp. 45–46.

78. Mein Kampf, p. 22.

79. Ibid., p. 180.

80. Ibid., pp. 184–88.

81. Joachim Fest, Hitler, trans. Richard and Clara Winston (New York, 1974), p. 36.

82.

83. Robert G. L. Waite, "Adolf Hitler's Anti-Semitism: A Study in History and Psychoanalysis," in The Psychoanalytic Interpretation of History, ed. Benjamin Wolsman (New York, 1971), p. 197.

84. Cornelius Tabori, My Occult Diary (London, 1951), p. 53.

85. Gerd-Klaus Kaltenbrunner, "Zwischen Rilke und Hitler-Alfred Schuler," Zeitschritt ffir Religions- und Geistesgeschichte 19 (1967): 338, 343.

86. Ibid.

87. Arad, Y., Gutman, I., Margaliot, A., Documents on the Holocaust, 8th Edition, United States, 1999.

88. Beevor, A., Stalingrad, London, 1998.

89. Brooker, P., Twentieth Century Dictatorships, London, 1995.

90. Carruthers, B. & Erickson, J., The Russian Front 1941–1945, London, 1999.

91. Halliday, F., Revolution and World Politics, London, 1999.

92. Kershaw, I., Hitler 1889–1936 Hubris, London, 1998.

93. Kershaw, I. Hitler 1936–1945 Nemesis, London 2000.

94. Wendel, M. The Third Reich Factbook, www.skalman.nu/third-reich/

95. Wendel, M. The Third Reich Forum, www.thirdreichforum.com

96. Kershaw, I.,Hitler 1889–1936 Hubris, London, 1998, pp. 170–171 #

97. ibid pp. 1731

98. Yitzhak Arad, Israel Gutman, Abraham Margaliot, Documents on the Holocaust, 8th Edition, United States, 1999, pp 15–18ll

99. Paul Brooker, Twentieth-Century Dictatorships, London, 1995, pp. 40l

100. Antony Beevor, Stalingrad, London, 1998, pp. 141

101. Ian Kershaw, Hitler 1936–1945 Nemesis, London, 2000, pp. 3531

102. ibid pp. 171

103. ibid pp.2411

104. Arad, pp. 376l

105. ibid pp. 3891

106. Compiled by Marcus Wendel, The Third Reich Factbookl

107. Kershaw, Nemesis, pp. 354–355l

108. ibid pp. 256l

109. Beevor, pp. 55l

110. Miller and Rupp, Nazi Ideology before 1933: A Documentation, 1978, pp. 11–36.

111. Weinstein, The Dynamics of Nazism, 1980,pp. 11–46.

Index

www.ingramcontent.com/pod-product-compliance
Lightning Source LLC
Chambersburg PA
CBHW021823270326
41932CB00007B/312